Stories of
HEAVENLY
MANSIONS
FROM THE VIMANAVATTHU

One of the books of the Pali Canon
Found in the Khuddaka Nikaya.

A translation into English from the Sinhala translation
by Most Venerable Kiribathgoda Gnānānanda Thera

A Mahamegha Publication

Stories of Heavenly Mansions from the Vimanavatthu
by Most Venerable Kiribathgoda Gnānānanda Thera

© All Rights Reserved

ISBN:9789556870541

1st Print: Nawam Full Moon Poyaday - 2556 B.E. (Feb. 2013)

Second Edition May 2015

Computer Typesetting by

Mahamevnawa Buddhist Monastery, Toronto
Markham, Ontario, Canada L6C 1P2
Telephone: 905-927-7117

Published by

Mahamegha Publishers
Waduwawa, Yatigaloluwa, Polgahawela, Sri Lanka.
Telephone: +94 37 2053300 | 77 3216685
www.mahameghapublishers.com
mahameghapublishers@gmail.com

Dedication

As there are lotuses that rise clear above the water and seek the nourishing beam of the sun, there are beings who seek the wisdom of the Supreme Buddha's Dhamma.

May they achieve the ultimate bliss of Nibbāna.

Lokavabodha Sutta

"Bhikkhus, the world has been fully understood by the Tathāgata; the Tathāgata is released from the world.

Bhikkhus, the origin of the world has been fully understood by the Tathāgata; the origin of the world has been eradicated by the Tathāgata.

Bhikkhus, the cessation of the world has been fully understood by the Tathāgata; the cessation of the world has been realized by the Tathāgata.

Bhikkhus, the path leading to the cessation of the world has been fully understood by the Tathāgata; the path leading to the cessation of the world has been developed by the Tathāgata.

Bhikkhus, in this world with its devas, māras and brahmās, with its recluses and brahmins, among humankind with its princes and people, whatever is seen, whatever is heard, whatever is smelled, whatever is tasted, whatever is touched, whatever is cognized, whatever is attained, whatever is sought, and whatever is comprehended, all have been fully understood by the Tathāgata. Thus, the Blessed One is called the Tathāgata.

Bhikkhus, from the night when the Tathāgata awakened to unsurpassed Supreme Enlightenment until the night when the Tathāgata passes away into Nibbāna, with nothing remaining, whatever the Tathāgata speaks, utters, and explains, all that is just so, and not otherwise. Thus, the Blessed One is called the Tathāgata.

Bhikkhus, as the Tathāgata says, so the Tathāgata does. As the Tathāgata does, so the Tathāgata says. In this way, as the Tathāgata says, so the Tathāgata does. As the Tathāgata does, so the Tathāgata says. Thus, the Blessed One is called the Tathāgata.

Bhikkhus, in this world, with its devas, māras, and brahmās, with its recluses and brahmins, among humankind with its princes and people, the Tathāgata is the conqueror, unvanquished, all-seer, wielding power. Thus, the Blessed One is called the Tathāgata."

This was said by the Blessed One. So, with regard to this, it was said:

By knowledge of the whole world, the whole world as it truly is, the Blessed One is released from all the world, in all the world the Blessed One is unattached.

The all-conquering heroic sage, freed from every bond is the Blessed One; the Blessed One has reached that perfect peace, Nibbāna which is free from fear.

Rid of taints, the Blessed One is enlightened, free from suffering, and free from doubts; he has destroyed all kamma, and is released by the full destruction of clinging.

Our Supreme Buddha, our Blessed One, is a lion, unsurpassed; for in the world together with its devas, the Blessed One set the Brahma-wheel in motion.

Thus those devas and human beings, gone for refuge to the Supreme Buddha, on meeting the Blessed One, pay homage — the Greatest One, free from diffidence.

Tamed, the Blessed One is unsurpassed in taming others. Calmed, the Blessed One is unsurpassed in calming others. Freed, the Blessed One is unsurpassed in freeing others. Crossed over, the Blessed One is unsurpassed in helping others to cross over.

Thus, they pay due homage to the Blessed One, the Greatest One free from diffidence, by saying:

"In the world together with its devas, there is no other equalling you, our Supreme Buddha."

Khuddaka Nikāya, Itv 112

All have I overcome, all-knowing am I;
with regard to all things, unattached.
Having renounced all,
and released in the end of craving;
having fully comprehended on my own,
whom shall I call 'my teacher'?

The gift of Dhamma surpasses all gifts;
the taste of Dhamma, all tastes;
delight in Dhamma, all delights.
One who has destroyed craving,
vanquishes all suffering.

Gautama Supreme Buddha
Dhp 353-354

Introduction

Meritorious Sons, Daughters, and Devotees,

We are very fortunate to learn about the knowledges of the Supreme Buddha. Our great teacher, the Supreme Buddha, had an extraordinary knowledge to see past lives of beings. In the Bhayaberava Sutta the Buddha tells us how he gained the knowledge to see his own past lives:

> When my mind was concentrated, purified, bright, clear, free from defilements, open, soft, steady, and unshakable, I directed my mind to the knowledge of recollecting my past lives. I recollected my various past lives, that is, one birth, two births... five, ten... fifty, a hundred, a thousand, a hundred thousand births, many eons of the cycle of formation and destruction of this earth. In one life I had such a name, belonged to such a clan, had such an appearance. Such was my food, such my experience of pleasure and pain, such the end of my life. Passing away from that life, I was reborn in another place. There too I had such a name, belonged to such a clan, had such an appearance. Such was my food, such my experience of pleasure and pain, such the end of my life. Passing away from that state, I was reborn here. I remembered my different past lives in every detail.

> This was the first knowledge I attained in the first watch of the night. My ignorance was destroyed, knowledge arose, darkness was destroyed, light arose, which happens in one who is mindful, passionate, and firm.

Next the Supreme Buddha gained the knowledge to see how other beings travel in this cycle of samsara, one life to another, because of their good and bad actions.

> When my mind was concentrated, purified, bright, clear, free from defilements, open, soft, steady, and unshakable, I directed my mind to gain the knowledge of the passing away and rebirth of beings. With my divine eye which is purified and surpassing the human eye, I saw beings passing away and re-appearing, and I discovered how they are inferior and superior, beautiful and ugly, fortunate and unfortunate in accordance with their kamma: beings who committed bad conduct of body, speech and mind, who insulted noble ones, held wrong views and did bad deeds because of it, with the break-up of their body, after death, have been reborn in a bad destination, the lower realms, in hell. But those beings who committed good deeds with body, speech, and mind, who did not insult noble ones, who held right views and did good deeds because of it, with the break-up of the body, after death, have been reborn in the good destinations, in the heavenly world. Therefore with my divine eye, which is purified and surpassing the human eye, I saw beings passing away and reborn, and I discovered how they are inferior and superior, beautiful and ugly, fortunate and unfortunate in accordance with their kamma.

The Supreme Buddha is the knower of all worlds. He knows the qualities of all the worlds and the way beings are born in these different worlds, as he explains in the Maha Sihanada Sutta:

> Sariputta, there are five types of beings. What are the five? Hell beings, animals, ghosts, human beings and gods.

> I understand hell, and the path and way leading to hell. And I also understand how people who will be born in hell, on the breaking up of the body, after death, reappear in a state of misery, in an unhappy destination, miserable, in hell.

> I understand the animal world, and the path and way leading to the animal world. And I also understand how one who has entered this path will, on the breaking up of the body, after death, be reborn as an animal.

> I understand the realm of ghosts, and the path and way leading to the realm of ghosts. And I also understand how one who has entered this path will, on the breaking up of the body, after death, reappear in the realm of ghosts.

> I understand human beings, and the path and way leading to the human world. And I also understand how one who has entered this path will, on the breaking up of the body, after death, reappear among human beings.

> I understand the gods, and the path and way leading to the world of the gods. And I also understand how one who has entered this path will, on the breaking up of the body, after death, reappear in a happy destination, in the heavenly world.

And most fortunately, noble disciples have the opportunity to escape from all worlds by attaining Nibbana. The Supreme Buddha is the only teacher to show the way to Nibbana.

> I understand Nibbana, and the path and way leading to Nibbana. I also understand how one who has entered this path will, by realizing it for himself with direct knowledge, here and now enter upon and abide in the liberation of the mind and liberation by wisdom that is taintless with the destruction of the taints.

From this book you are going to learn the actions that lead to the heavenly world and how beings are rejoicing living as devas. You will notice that they all lived in the human world like we do now. Here, the Supreme Buddha explains the happiness of the heavenly world with a simile:

> By investigating a person's mind using my psychic powers I understand how that person behaves. This person having behaved in such a way, on the dissolution of the body, after death, will reappear in a heavenly realm. Later on, I see that he has reappeared in a heavenly realm and is experiencing exclusively pleasant feelings. Suppose there was mansion and it had an upper room plastered inside and out, closed off, protected, with shutters on the windows. It had a couch with blankets and sheets, spread with a deer skin, covered by a canopy and with red pillows at both ends. Then a man, burnt and exhausted by hot weather, tired, dry and thirsty, headed to that place in hopes of resting in the mansion. A wise person then sees the

thirsty man who has taken the path towards
the mansion and realizes that the path that man
is on will lead him to that mansion.

Read these stories very carefully. Think about your own
life and how you can apply the lessons these devas have
learned from their good behavior in the human world.
May these stories help you to develop a desire to do
wholesome actions in your precious human life.

May you practice generosity. May you keep the precepts
well. May you control your bad thoughts. By practicing
Dhamma, may you attain rebirth in the heavenly worlds.

May all of you realize the Four Noble Truths in this
Gautama Buddha's Dispensation.

With metta,

Kiribathgoda Gnanananda Bhikkhu

Mahamevnawa Monastery
Waduwawa, Yatigaloluwa, Polgahawela
Sri Lanka
Buddhist Year 2556 (2013)

Contents

3. The Coral Tree Chapter

4. The Crimson Chapter

7. The Sunikkhitta Chapter

Namo Tassa Bhagavato Arahato
Sammā Sambuddhassa!

Homage to the Blessed One, the Worthy One,
the Supremely Enlightened One!

1. The Seats Chapter

1.1 Throne Mansion

Moggallana Bhante:

Dear Devata, you are sitting on a golden throne. It flies wherever you want, and as quickly as you want it to. You are beautifully dressed, wearing garlands of flowers, and you are radiant, like lightning shining through the clouds.

What kind of meritorious action did you do when you were in the human world to have gained this beauty that shines in all directions, and to have earned all these wonderful things?

That devata, delighted at being questioned by Arahant Moggallana, gladly explained what she had done that resulted in such great happiness.

Devata:

Bhante, when I was in the human world, a monk visited our house and I prepared a chair for him to sit on. Raising my hands and putting my palms and fingers together, I saluted that monk respectfully. I also offered almsfood to him.

Because of these meritorious deeds, I have been born as a very beautiful devata and enjoy all the wonderful things that delight my heart.

Great Bhante, these are the meritorious deeds I did to have such a beautiful body that shines in all directions.

1.2 Second Throne Mansion

Moggallana Bhante:

Dear Devata, you are sitting on a throne made of beryl gemstones. It flies wherever you want, and as quickly as you want it to. You are beautifully dressed, wearing garlands of flowers, and you are radiant, like lightning shining through the clouds.

What kind of meritorious action did you do when you were in the human world to have gained this beauty that shines in all directions, and to have earned all these wonderful things?

That devata, delighted at being questioned by Arahant Moggallana, gladly explained what she had done that resulted in such great happiness.

Devata:

Bhante, when I was in the human world, a monk visited our house and I prepared a chair for him to sit on. Raising my hands and putting my palms and fingers together, I saluted that monk respectfully. I also offered almsfood to him.

Because of these meritorious deeds, I have been born as a very beautiful devata and enjoy all the wonderful things that delight my heart.

Great Bhante, these are the meritorious deeds I did to have such a beautiful body that shines in all directions.

1.3 Third Throne Mansion

Moggallana Bhante:

Dear Devata, you are sitting on a golden throne. It flies wherever you want, and as quickly as you want it to. You are beautifully dressed, wearing garlands of flowers, and you are radiant, like lightning shining through the clouds.

What kind of meritorious action did you do when you were in the human world to have gained this beauty that shines in all directions, and to have earned all these wonderful things?

That devata, delighted at being questioned by Arahant Moggallana, gladly explained what she had done that resulted in such great happiness.

Devata:
Bhante, when I was in the human world I did a very small meritorious act. One day, I saw a monk without defilements, calm in mind, free from agitation. My mind was pleased at the sight of that monk; I had great confidence in him. I offered him a chair that I had prepared with my own hands.

Because of this meritorious deed, I have been born as a very beautiful devata and enjoy all the wonderful things that delight my heart.

Great Bhante, that is the meritorious action I did to have such a beautiful body that shines in all directions.

1.4 Fourth Throne Mansion

Moggallana Bhante:
Dear Devata, you are sitting on a throne made of beryl gemstones. It flies wherever you want, and as quickly as you want it to. You are beautifully dressed, wearing garlands of flowers, and you are radiant, like lightning shining through the clouds.

What kind of meritorious action did you do when you were in the human world to have gained this beauty that shines in all directions, and to have earned all these wonderful things?

That devata, delighted at being questioned by Arahant Moggallana, gladly explained what she had done that resulted in such great happiness.

Devata:

Bhante, when I was in the human world I did a very small meritorious act. One day, I saw a monk without defilements, calm in mind, free from agitation. My mind was pleased at the sight of that monk; I had great confidence in him. I offered him a chair that I had prepared with my own hands.

Because of this meritorious deed, I have been born as a very beautiful devata and enjoy all the wonderful things that delight my heart.

Great Bhante, that is the meritorious action I did to have such a beautiful body that shines in all directions.

1.5 Elephant Mansion

Moggallana Bhante:

Devata, your mansion is a divine elephant decorated with various jewels. It is pleasing and powerful. It is very fast and moves smoothly through the air.

Your eyes are as beautiful as lotus petals. The color of your elephant is like blue and red lotuses. Its whole body is covered with lotus powder and it is wearing lotus garlands made of gold.

Your elephant travels over a road that is covered in lotus flowers and leaves. The way your elephant walks is charming and pleasing. As it steps forward, golden bells, sweet in tone, are heard. The sound is like an orchestra.

As you are seated on that great elephant's back, decorated and wearing divine clothes, your beauty is greater than all the other devas.

Is all this the fruit of your generosity, your virtuous behavior, or because you worshiped monks in the past? Please answer my questions, so that I may know.

That devata, delighted at being questioned by Arahant Moggallana, gladly explained what she had done that resulted in such great happiness.

Devata:
Bhante, one day I saw a monk who meditated frequently and had very noble qualities. I offered him a chair covered with cloth and lotus flowers. Using lotus garlands and flowers, I decorated the floor around the chair with my own hands.

As a result of these meritorious deeds, I have received these wonderful things. I am treated with great care and respected in this heavenly world and I am honored by the other devas.

Surely, if someone with a confident heart offers a seat to those who are free from defilements and are calm in mind, that person will experience great happiness, just as I do now.

Someone who cares about his own well-being and who wants to experience good results should offer seats to Arahants who are in their final body.

1.6 Ship Mansion

Moggallana Bhante:

Devata, your divine mansion is a ship with a roof made of gold. It floats on a pond filled with lotus flowers. You happily pick those lotus flowers with your own hands.

What kind of meritorious action did you do when you were in the human world to have gained this beauty that shines in all directions, and to have earned all these wonderful things?

That devata, delighted at being questioned by Arahant Moggallana, gladly explained what she had done that resulted in such great happiness.

Devata:

In my previous life I was a woman in the human world. One day, I saw several monks who were very thirsty and had fallen to the ground. I got up quickly and offered them water to drink.

Now I know if people offer water to a monk who is thirsty, cool ponds full of white lotuses will appear for them in the heavenly world. Further, their divine mansions will be surrounded with beautiful sandy beaches where streams of water flow smoothly. Mango trees, sala trees, tilakas, rose apples, cassias and trumpet flowers will be in full bloom everywhere. These beautiful mansions appear in such places. They shine brilliantly.

Bhante, that was my meritorious deed which gave me this wonderful result. Only those who do meritorious deeds deserve this happiness.

Because of this meritorious deed, I have been born as a very beautiful devata and enjoy all the wonderful things that delight my heart.

Great Bhante, that is the meritorious action I did to have such a beautiful body that shines in all directions.

1.7 Second Ship Mansion

Moggallana Bhante:
Devata, your divine mansion is a ship with a roof made of gold. It floats on a pond filled with lotus flowers. You happily pick those lotus flowers with your own hands.

What kind of meritorious action did you do when you were in the human world to have gained this beauty that shines in all directions, and to have earned all these wonderful things?

That devata, delighted at being questioned by Arahant Moggallana, gladly explained what she had done that resulted in such great happiness.

Devata:
In my previous life I was a woman in the human world. One day, I saw a monk who was very thirsty and had fallen to the ground. I got up quickly and offered him water to drink.

Now I know if people offer water to a monk who is thirsty, cool ponds full of white lotuses will appear for them in the heavenly world. Furthermore, their divine mansions will be surrounded with beautiful sandy beaches where streams of water flow smoothly. Mango trees, sala trees, tilakas, rose apples, cassias and trumpet flowers will be in full bloom everywhere. These beautiful mansions appear in such places. They shine brilliantly.

Bhante, that was my meritorious deed which gave me this wonderful result. Only those who do meritorious deeds deserve this happiness.

Because of this meritorious deed, I have been born as a very beautiful devata and enjoy all the wonderful things that delight my heart.

Great Bhante, that is the meritorious action I did to have such a beautiful body that shines in all directions.

1.8 Third Ship Mansion

Supreme Buddha:

Devata, your divine mansion is a ship with a roof made of gold. It floats on a pond that is filled with lotus flowers. You happily pick those lotus flowers with your own hands.

Your divine mansion is huge and is separated into many different rooms. It shines in all directions.

What kind of meritorious action did you do when you were in the human world to have gained this beauty that shines in all directions, and to have earned all these wonderful things?

That devata, delighted at being questioned by the Supreme Buddha, gladly explained what she had done that resulted in such great happiness.

Devata:

In my previous life I was a woman in the human world. One day, I saw several monks who were very thirsty and had fallen to the ground. I got up quickly and offered them water to drink.

Now I know if people offer water to a monk who is thirsty, cool ponds full of white lotuses will appear for them in the heavenly world. Furthermore, their divine mansions will be surrounded with beautiful sandy beaches where streams of water flow smoothly. Mango trees, sala trees, tilakas, rose apples, cassias and trumpet flowers will be in full bloom everywhere. These beautiful mansions appear in such places. They shine brilliantly.

Bhante, that was my meritorious deed which gave me this wonderful result. Only those who do meritorious deeds deserve this happiness.

Because of this meritorious deed, I have been born as a very beautiful devata and enjoy all the wonderful things that delight my heart.

Great Bhante, that is the meritorious action I did to have such a beautiful body that shines in all directions.

1.9 Lamp Mansion

Moggallana Bhante:

Devata, your beauty shines in all directions like the bright star named Osadhi.

What are the meritorious deeds you have done to gain this happiness?

Devata, the pure radiance of your body and limbs is stainless and shines in all directions.

What kind of meritorious action did you do when you were in the human world to have gained this beauty that shines in all directions, and to have earned all these wonderful things?

That devata, delighted at being questioned by Arahant Moggallana, gladly explained what she had done that resulted in such great happiness.

Devata:

In my previous life, I was a woman in the human world. One night, there was a certain area which was very dark. People desperately needed light there. I lighted that area with a lamp.

Now I know for certian, if someone provides lamps to light a dark area, that person is reborn in the heavenly mansion called Jotirasa. There are beautiful flowers there like white lotuses.

Because of this meritorious deed, I have been born as a very beautiful devata and enjoy all the wonderful things that delight my heart.

That is why the pure radiance of my body and limbs is stainless and shines in all directions.

Great Bhante, that is the meritorious action I did to have such a beautiful body that shines in all directions.

1.10 Sesame-Gift Mansion

Moggallana Bhante:

Devata, your beauty shines in all directions like the bright star named Osadhi.

What are the meritorious deeds that led to this happiness?

Devata, the pure radiance of your body and limbs is stainless and shines in all directions.

Tell me Devata, what kind of meritorious action did you do when you were in the human world to have gained this beauty that shines in all directions, and to have earned all these wonderful things?

That devata, delighted at being questioned by Arahant Moggallana, gladly explained what she had done that resulted in such great happiness.

Devata:

In my previous life, I was a woman in the human world. One day I saw the Supreme Buddha who was free from defilements and had a peaceful mind. I knew very well that the Buddha was worthy of gifts and therefore my mind had confidence in him. I was a little worried because I did not have valuable things to offer. But still, I offered some sesame seeds with my own hands.

Because of this meritorious deed, I have been born as a very beautiful devata and enjoy all the wonderful things that delight my heart.

Great Bhante, that is the meritorious action I did to have such a beautiful body that shines in all directions.

1.11 Honest Wife Mansion

Moggallana Bhante:

Dear Devata, your mansion is very beautiful. It is decorated with all kinds of flowers. Divine herons, peacocks, geese, and sweet-voiced cuckoos fly around the mansion. Pretty gods and goddesses are always dancing and singing to entertain you.

Devata, you are very mighty, possessing many kinds of psychic powers. Tell me Devata, what kind of meritorious action did you do when you were in the human world to have gained this beauty that shines in all directions, and to have earned all these wonderful things?

That devata, delighted at being questioned by Arahant Moggallana, gladly explained what she had done that resulted in such great happiness.

Devata:

In my previous life, I was a woman in the human world. I was a very honest and faithful wife. I never had a desire for someone else's husband. I protected my husband like a mother protects her only child. There were times that I got angry, but I never spoke harshly to him.

I never told lies; lying was not a part of my life. I delighted in giving and sharing. I practiced generosity with a happy mind. I offered food and drink with respect.

Because of these meritorious deeds, I have been born as a very beautiful devata and enjoy all the wonderful things that delight my heart.

Great Bhante, these are the meritorious deeds I did to have such a beautiful body that shines in all directions.

1.12 Second Honest Wife Mansion

Moggallana Bhante:

Dear Devata, your mansion is very beautiful. It is decorated with various carvings made of beryl and other gemstones. Pretty gods and goddesses are always dancing and singing to entertain you.

Devata, you are very mighty, possessing various kinds of psychic powers.

Tell me Devata, what kind of meritorious action did you do when you were in the human world to have gained this beauty that shines in all directions, and to have earned all these wonderful things?

That devata, delighted at being questioned by Arahant Moggallana, gladly explained what she had done that resulted in such great happiness.

Devata:
In my previous life, I was a woman in the human world, a lay disciple of the very wise Supreme Buddha.

I abstained from killing, stealing, taking intoxicants, and lying. I was content with my own husband and did not want to think of other men. I practiced generosity with a happy mind. I offered food and drink with respect.

Because of these meritorious deeds, I have been born as a very beautiful devata and enjoy all the wonderful things that delight my heart.

Great Bhante, those were the meritorious deeds I did to have such a beautiful body that shines in all directions.

1.13 Daughter-in-Law Mansion

Moggallana Bhante:
Devata, your beauty shines in all directions like the bright star named Osadhi.

What are the meritorious deeds that led to this happiness?

Tell me Devata, what kind of meritorious action did you do when you were in the human world to have gained this beauty that shines in all directions, and to have earned all these wonderful things?

That devata, delighted at being questioned by Arahant Moggallana, gladly explained what she had done that resulted in such great happiness.

Devata:

In my previous life, I was a woman in the human world, a daughter-in-law living in my father-in-law's house. One day I was pleased to see a monk who was free from defilements and had a peaceful mind.

I had two oil cakes and happily offered one to the monk with my own hands. To my amazement, I was reborn in the heavenly Nandana Park as a goddess.

Because of this meritorious deed, I have been born as a very beautiful devata and enjoy all the wonderful things that delight my heart.

Great Bhante, that was the meritorious action I did to have such a beautiful body that shines in all directions.

1.14 Second Daughter-in-Law Mansion

Moggallana Bhante:
Devata, your beauty shines in all directions like the bright star named Osadhi.

What are the meritorious deeds that led to this happiness?

Tell me Devata, what kind of meritorious action did you do when you were in the human world to have gained this beauty that shines in all directions, and to have earned all these wonderful things?

That devata, delighted at being questioned by Arahant Moggallana, gladly explained what she had done that resulted in such great happiness.

Devata:
In my previous life, I was a woman in the human world, a daughter-in-law living in my father-in-law's house.

One day I was pleased to see a monk who was free from defilements and had a peaceful mind.

I offered a honey-covered cake to that monk. To my amazement, I was reborn in the heavenly Nandana Park as a goddess.

Because of this meritorious deed, I have been born as a very beautiful devata and enjoy all the wonderful things that delight my heart.

Great Bhante, that was the meritorious action I did to have such a beautiful body that shines in all directions.

1.15 Uttara's Mansion

Moggallana Bhante:
Devata, your beauty shines in all directions like the bright star named Osadhi.

What are the meritorious deeds that led to this happiness?

Tell me Devata, what kind of meritorious action did you do when you were in the human world to have gained this beauty that shines in all directions, and to have earned all these wonderful things?

That devata, delighted at being questioned by Arahant Moggallana, gladly explained what she had done that resulted in such great happiness.

Devata:
In my previous life, I was a housewife in the human world. I did not envy anyone. I was not greedy, nor was I arrogant. I was obedient to my husband and did not get angry at him. I was eager to observe the Eight Precepts four times a month on each of the four moon phases. I led a restrained life and was very generous.

I abstained from killing, stealing, lying, and taking intoxicants. I did not cheat on my husband. I was delighted to keep these Five Precepts every day. I was a lay follower of Gautama Supreme Buddha who had the great wisdom to see the reality of the world. I was wise enough to realize the Four Noble Truths.

Because of my virtuous life and meritorious deeds, I live very happily here. I have been born as a beautiful devata and enjoy all the wonderful things that delight my heart.

Great Bhante, those were the meritorious deeds I did to have such a beautiful body that shines in all directions.

Please Bhante, pay homage on my behalf by placing your head on the Blessed One's sacred feet and saying, "Bhante, the lay follower named Uttara pays homage by placing her head on the Blessed One's sacred feet." The Blessed One stated that I have attained a certain fruit of enlightenment. I too know that.

Bhante, the Supreme Buddha declared that I have attained the fruit of once returner.

1.16 Sirima's Mansion

Vangisa Bhante:
Devata, your chariot is very beautiful. The divine horses that pull it are very powerful and fast, and they are decorated with various ornaments. These horses travel down through the sky. Just as horses obey their driver, these horses take you to wherever your mind wishes to go. You have received five hundred chariots. Is this not the result of a powerful act of merit?

While you sit in the chariot decorated with ornaments, you shine like a fire which provides bright light. Devata, you are extremely beautiful. From which heavenly world did you come here to visit the Supreme Buddha?

Devata:

Bhante, the heavenly world that I came from is a great place even amongst the other heavenly worlds. There the gods create whatever divine pleasures they wish for and delight in their creation. I am a goddess from that heaven and I too have created various wonderful things according to my wish. I have come from that heaven to pay homage to the Supreme Buddha.

Vangisa Bhante:

Devata, you possess psychic powers and your body illuminates all the directions. Surrounded and respected by many gods, you are traveling through the sky. Tell me where you lived before you were born as a goddess. Whose teaching did you follow? Are you a follower of the Supreme Buddha? What kind of meritorious actions did you do in the past?

Devata:

In the human world there once was a beautiful city called Rajagaha surrounded by five mountains. I was a queen of the famous king Bimbisara. I was very talented in dancing and singing. Everyone knew me as Sirima.

The Supreme Buddha is a great teacher. He is very skilled at training gods and humans. My great teacher, the Supreme Buddha, taught me the Four Noble Truths. He taught that suffering and the cause of suffering are impermanent. He taught me the end of suffering, Nibbana, which is unconditioned and unchanging. And he taught me the Noble Eightfold Path which is a straight and excellent way leading to the end of suffering.

Having learned about the bliss of Nibbana from the unsurpassed teacher, the Supreme Buddha, I had great confidence in that teaching. I kept the precepts well and led a very restrained life.

I recognized the true way to Nibbana and understood clearly the teachings of the Supreme Buddha. I developed concentration through serene meditation. That concentration became a key factor of my practice.

I realized the Four Noble Truths. I am free from doubt in the teachings. Many gods honor me and I enjoy many wonderful things here.

I am a follower of the wisest teacher, the Supreme Buddha, and I am headed to Nibbana. Through the realization of the Four Noble Truths, I have reached the first stage of enlightenment, the fruit of stream entry. I have escaped from all bad destinations.

I came to worship my great teacher, the Supreme Buddha. The sight of virtuous monks is also pleasing to me and I worship them happily.

The most supreme, matchless trainer of beings, the Supreme Buddha, has cut off all cravings and delights in Nibbana. The Blessed One is compassionate to all beings. Even just seeing the Buddha is delightful. My happiness is beyond words. I pay homage to my great teacher, the Supreme Buddha.

1.17 Kesakari's Mansion

Devata:
My mansion is very beautiful and shines in all directions. The pillars of the mansion are made of beryl gemstones.

Golden trees decorate the surrounding garden. This mansion appeared as a result of my meritorious deeds.

God Sakka:

One hundred thousand goddesses were born before you here in this mansion to be your attendants. Now you enjoy their company and their service. The light of the full moon shines and surpasses the stars in brightness. The same goes for you: you shine brilliantly and surpass all the other goddesses. Your appearance is extraordinary.

All the gods in Tavatimsa Heaven, headed by me, are overcome with the desire to stare at the great Brahma and admire him. They cannot help but stare at him. So too, is your appearance. All the gods stare at you and admire you. Please tell me where you have come from. In which world did you live in before you were born here?

Devata:

God Sakka, I will tell you everything. In the human world, there is a city called Baranasi in the state of Kasi. I was a woman in that city and my name was Kesakarika. I had great confidence in the Supreme Buddha, the Dhamma, and the Noble Sangha. My faith in the Triple Gem was unshakable. All my doubts were removed. I kept the Five Precepts very purely and I attained the fruit of stream entry. As a result, I am surely headed to the realization of Nibbana.

God Sakka:

Excellent! You have great confidence in the Supreme Buddha, the Dhamma, and the Noble Sangha. Your faith in the Triple Gem is unshakable. All your doubts are removed. You lived under the Five Precepts very purely and you have attained the fruit of stream entry.

As a result, you are surely heading to the realization of Nibbana.

Devata, you shine due to your Dhamma practice and your retinue of goddesses. You are greatly welcomed here in this world. We rejoice in your arrival here.

2. The Cittalata Chapter

2.1 Servant Girl's Mansion

Moggallana Bhante:
Devata, just like the god Sakka, you walk around here in Cittalata Park surrounded by many goddesses. Your beauty shines in all directions like the bright star named Osadhi.

What are the meritorious deeds that led to this happiness?

Tell me Devata, what kind of meritorious actions did you do when you were in the human world to have gained this beauty that shines in all directions, and to have earned all these wonderful things?

That devata, delighted at being questioned by Arahant Moggallana, gladly explained what she had done that resulted in such great happiness.

Devata:
Bhante, in my previous life I was a girl in the human world. I was a servant working in other people's houses. I was very fortunate to be a lay follower of the Supreme Buddha. Gautama Supreme Buddha knew everything about the world. Nothing could shake his peace of mind. Following my great teacher's instructions, all I wished for was to escape from this cycle of birth and death.

I will try my best to practice the Dhamma. Even when my body breaks up, I will not give up my effort. This excellent path to Nibbana was discovered by the Supreme Buddhas. This is a straight, secure, and pure path. This Dhamma path leading to Nibbana includes the Five Precepts. Even though I am a woman, you will see how committed I am to achieve the result of the path.

Even the powerful god Sakka invites me to his entertaining events. Sixty thousand musical instruments are played to wake me from my sleep. Many gods such as Alamba, Gaggara, Bhima, Sadhuvadin, Samsaya, Pokkhara, and Suphassa and many goddesses such as Vinamokkha, Nanda, Sunanda, Sonadinna, Sucimhita, Alambusa, Missakesi, Pundarika, Eniphassa, Suphassa, Subhadda, and Muduvadini entertain me by playing music. They come into my presence whenever I wish and delight me by saying, "Let's dance now! Let's sing now!"

Only those who have done meritorious deeds can enjoy this heavenly Nandana Park in the sorrowless Tavatimsa Heaven, not those who did no meritorious deeds. Doers of good enjoy happiness in this life and the next, but doers of evil will receive unhappiness in this life and the next.

Anyone who would like to join us in the Tavatimsa Heaven must do lots of wholesome deeds. Only those who do good deeds are reborn in heaven and enjoy divine entertainment.

2.2 Lakhuma's Mansion

Moggallana Bhante:
Devata, you are in this Cittalata Park surrounded by many goddesses as if you were the god Sakka. Your beauty shines in all directions like the bright star named Osadhi.

What are the meritorious deeds that led to this happiness?

Tell me Devata, what kind of meritorious actions did you do when you were in the human world to have gained this beauty that shines in all directions, and to have earned all these wonderful things?

That devata, delighted at being questioned by Arahant Moggallana, gladly explained what she had done that resulted in such great happiness.

Devata:
Bhante, in the human world my house was located in a fishing village. Some of the Supreme Buddha'a monks visited that area for almsround. With a happy mind, I offered rice, honey-covered cake, vegetables, and rice-gruel to those virtuous monks who were dedicated to Dhamma practice.

I was eager to observe the Eight Precepts four times a month on each of the four moon phases. I led a restrained life and was very generous.

I abstained from killing, stealing, lying, and taking intoxicants. I did not cheat on my husband. I was delighted to keep these Five Precepts every day. I was a lay follower of Gautama Supreme Buddha, the one who had the great wisdom to see the reality of the world. I was wise enough to realize the Four Noble Truths.

Because of my virtuous life and meritorious deeds, I live happily here. I have been born as a very beautiful devata and enjoy all the wonderful things that delight my heart.

Great Bhante, those were the meritorious deeds I did to have such a beautiful body that shines in all directions.

Please Bhante, pay homage on my behalf by placing your head on the Blessed One's feet and saying, "Bhante, the lay follower named Lakhuma pays homage by placing her head on the Blessed One's feet." The Blessed One stated that I have attained a certain fruit of enlightenment. I too know that.

Bhante, the Supreme Buddha declared that I have attained the fruit of once returner.

2.3 Rice-Crust Giver's Mansion

God Sakka:

Kassapa Bhante, do you remember one day while you were on your almsround, you stood silently in front of a certain house? In that house there was a very poor lady of a low caste who used to go to other people's houses to beg for food.

She was very pleased when she saw you and offered some rice-crust with her own hands. Now that she has died, which world was she reborn in?

Kassapa Bhante:

God Sakka, yes I do remember that day when I was on my almsround and I stood silently in front of a certain house. In that house there was a very poor lady of a low caste who used to go to other people's houses to beg for food.

She was very pleased when she saw me and she offered some rice-crust with her own hands. Now she has died and escaped from that painful human life. She has been reborn in Nimmanarati Heaven where all the mighty devas possess psychic powers. That lady who offered some rice-crust now enjoys heavenly pleasures there.

God Sakka:

Amazing! It is wonderful! That poor lady offered rice-crust to Arahant Kassapa Bhante which she had begged from others, and that offering generated a wonderful result.

If one becomes the beautiful queen of a wheel-turning monarch, the happiness she experiences is not even worth a sixteenth part of the result of this rice-crust gift.

A hundred gold coins, a hundred horses, a hundred chariots pulled by mules, a hundred thousand maidens decorated in beautiful ornaments—happiness gained from these items is not worth a sixteenth part of the result of this rice-crust gift.

Even the happiness gained from a hundred Himalayan elephants with round tusks like wheels and necks decorated with golden ornaments is not worth a sixteenth part of the result of this rice-crust gift.

Even if someone became the ruler of this whole earth, a wheel-turning monarch, even his happiness is not worth a sixteenth part of the result of this rice-crust gift.

2.4 Low-Caste Woman's Mansion

Supreme Buddha:
Lady, I am Gautama Supreme Buddha standing before you out of compassion. I am the seventh Buddha who has appeared in the last hundred eons. Worship the feet of the famous Buddha. I am an Arahant and I am not shaken by the ups and downs of life. Let your mind be confident in me. Worship me immediately because you have little time to live.

In this way, the Supreme Buddha, with a developed mind and in his final body, encouraged the low-caste woman to collect merit. Having understood the words of the famous Gautama Buddha, she worshiped his sacred feet.

This world is covered with the darkness of ignorance. It is illuminated only by the true sunlight called the Four Noble Truths. She worshipped that Supreme Buddha who gives true light to the world.

Worshiping by putting her hands together, the woman gazed at the Buddha as he walked away. Soon after that, a cow attacked her and she died instantly.

Devata:
Oh Pure One, Arahant, Great Hero, the Supreme Buddha who meditates alone in the forest. I was born in heaven. Now I have come here to worship you.

Supreme Buddha:
Devata, you shine like gold and are surrounded by many goddesses. Having climbed down from your mansion, you worship me. Who are you?

Devata:
Bhante, I was a low-caste woman in the human world. Great Hero, Gautama Buddha, you encouraged me to collect merit. I worshiped your sacred feet. After my death, I was born in a divine mansion in Nandana Park

This mansion is extremely beautiful. I have one hundred thousand goddesses as my attendants. I surpass all of them in beauty, fame, and long life. Bhante, I did lots of good deeds with mindfulness and full awareness. Now I have come here to worship you, the compassionate Supreme Buddha.

The devata was very grateful. She recalled the Supreme Buddha's compassionate help. Having explained how she went to heaven, she worshiped the sacred feet of the Supreme Buddha and disappeared.

2.5 Lovely Lady's Mansion

Supreme Buddha:

Devata, around your mansion there are very beautiful mandarava trees and they are covered with blue, yellow, black, crimson, and red flower filaments. You are wearing a garland of mandarava flowers on your head. This beautiful type of tree is not found in any other heaven.

Famous devata, what meritorious deed did you do to be reborn in the Tavatimsa Heaven?

Devata:

Bhante, in the human world there is a city called Kimbila. There I was a female lay follower of the Supreme Buddha. My name was Bhadditthi. I had unshakable faith in the Triple Gem. I practiced the precepts and delighted in giving and sharing. Furthermore, I had confidence in noble monks who had pure minds. I offered robes, food, shelter, and lamps.

I was eager to observe the Eight Precepts four times a month on each of the four moon phases. I led a restrained life and was very generous.

I abstained from killing, stealing, lying, and taking intoxicants. I did not cheat on my husband. I was delighted to keep these Five Precepts every day. I was wise enough to realize the Four Noble Truths. That is how I became a dedicated follower of Gautama Supreme Buddha.

The compassionate sages, Arahant Sariputta and Arahant Moggallana, are the two chief disciples of the Supreme Buddha. One day I offered alms to them and collected lots of merit from that offering. I also observed the Eight Precepts four times a month frequently. As a result, when I left the human world, I was reborn in this heaven. Now I enjoy divine pleasures in the heavenly Nandana Park. My beauty radiates in all directions.

2.6 Sonadinna's Mansion

Moggallana Bhante:
Devata, your beauty shines in all directions like the bright star named Osadhi.

What meritorious deeds have you have done to gain this happiness?

Tell me Devata, what kind of meritorious action did you do when you were in the human world to have gained this beauty that shines in all directions, and to have earned all these wonderful things?

That devata, delighted at being questioned by Arahant Moggallana, gladly explained what she had done that resulted in such great happiness.

Devata:
Bhante, in the human world there is a city called Nalanda. There I was a female lay follower of the Supreme Buddha. My name was Sonadinna. I had unshakable faith in the Triple Gem. I practiced the precepts and delighted in giving and sharing. Furthermore, I had confidence in monks who had pure minds. I offered robes, food, shelter, and lamps to them.

I was eager to observe the Eight Precepts four times a month on each of the four moon phases. I led a restrained life and was very generous.

I abstained from killing, stealing, lying, and taking intoxicants. I did not cheat on my husband. I was delighted to keep these Five Precepts every day. I was wise enough to realize the Four Noble Truths. That is how I became a dedicated follower of Gautama Supreme Buddha.

Because of those meritorious deeds, I have been born as a very beautiful devata and enjoy all the wonderful things that delight my heart.

Great Bhante, those were the meritorious deeds I did to have such a beautiful body that shines in all directions.

2.7 Uposatha's Mansion

Moggallana Bhante:
Devata, your beauty shines in all directions like the bright star named Osadhi.

What are the meritorious deeds that led to this happiness?

Tell me Devata, what kind of meritorious action did you do when you were in the human world to have gained this beauty that shines in all directions, and to have earned all these wonderful things?

That devata, delighted at being questioned by Arahant Moggallana, gladly explained what she had done that resulted in such great happiness.

Devata:
Bhante, in the human world there is a city called Saketa. There I was a female lay follower of the Supreme Buddha. My name was Uposatha. I had unshakable faith in the Triple Gem. I practiced the precepts and delighted in giving and sharing. Furthermore, I had confidence in

noble monks who had pure minds. I offered them robes, food, shelter, and lamps.

I was eager to observe the Eight Precepts four times a month on each of the four moon phases. I led a restrained life and was very generous.

I abstained from killing, stealing, lying, and taking intoxicants. I did not cheat on my husband. I was delighted to keep these Five Precepts every day. I was wise enough to realize the Four Noble Truths. That is how I became a dedicated follower of Gautama Supreme Buddha.

Because of those meritorious deeds, I have been born as a very beautiful devata and enjoy all the wonderful things that delight my heart.

Great Bhante, those were the meritorious deeds I did to have such a beautiful body that shines in all directions.

When I was in the human world, I often heard stories about the heavenly Nandana Park. I had a desire to be born there. As a result of directing my mind to that park, I have been born here in this Tavatimsa Heaven.

My great teacher, the Supreme Buddha, who was born in the Clan of the Sun, frequently advised his disciples to achieve the highest stage of enlightenment they can. But I did not follow my great teacher's advice. Since I directed my mind to this inferior sensual realm, I was born in this heaven. I could have developed my mind further. Now I am sad and regret my decision.

Moggallana Bhante:
Devata, how long will you live in this mansion? Can you tell me your lifespan?

Devata:
Bhante, My lifespan here is three hundred million and sixty thousand years. After I pass away from here I will be reborn in the human world.

Moggallana Bhante:
Why fear, Uposatha? The Supreme Buddha has already stated that you have attained the fruit of stream entry. You will never again be born in a bad world.

2.8 Saddha's Mansion

Moggallana Bhante:
Devata, your beauty shines in all directions like the bright star named Osadhi.

What are the meritorious deeds that led to this happiness?

Tell me Devata, what kind of meritorious actions did you do when you were in the human world to have gained this beauty that shines in all directions, and to have earned all these wonderful things?

That devata, delighted at being questioned by Arahant Moggallana, gladly explained what she had done that resulted in such great happiness.

Devata:
Bhante, in the human world there is a city called Rajagaha. There I was a female lay follower of the Supreme Buddha. My name was Saddha. I had unshakable faith in the Triple Gem. I practiced the precepts and delighted in giving and sharing. Furthermore, I had confidence in noble monks who had pure minds. I offered robes, food, shelter, and lamps to them.

I was eager to observe the Eight Precepts four times a month on each of the four moon phases. I led a restrained life and was very generous.

I abstained from killing, stealing, lying, and taking intoxicants. I did not cheat on my husband. I was delighted to keep these Five Precepts every day. I was wise enough to realize the Four Noble Truths. That is how I became a dedicated follower of Gautama Supreme Buddha.

Because of these meritorious deeds, I have been born as a very beautiful devata and enjoy all the wonderful things that delight my heart.

Great Bhante, those were the meritorious deeds I did to have such a beautiful body that shines in all directions.

2.9 Sunanda's Mansion

Moggallana Bhante:
Devata, your beauty shines in all directions like the bright star named Osadhi.

What are the meritorious deeds that led to this happiness?

Tell me, Devata, what kind of meritorious action did you do when you were in the human world to have gained this beauty that shines in all directions, and to have earned all these wonderful things?

That devata, delighted at being questioned by Arahant Moggallana, gladly explained what she had done that resulted in such great happiness.

Devata:
Bhante, in the human world there is a city called Rajagaha. There I was a female lay follower of the Supreme Buddha.

My name was Sunanda. I had unshakable faith in the Triple Gem. I practiced the precepts and delighted in giving and sharing. Furthermore, I had confidence in noble monks who had pure minds. I offered robes, food, shelter, and lamps to them.

I was eager to observe the Eight Precepts four times a month on each of the four moon phases. I led a restrained life and was very generous.

I abstained from killing, stealing, lying, and taking intoxicants. I did not cheat on my husband. I delighted in keeping these Five Precepts every day. I was wise enough to realize the Four Noble Truths. That is how I became a dedicated follower of Gautama Supreme Buddha.

Because of these meritorious deeds, I have been born as a very beautiful devata and enjoy all the wonderful things that delight my heart.

Great Bhante, those were the meritorious deeds I did to have such a beautiful body that shines in all directions.

2.10 Alms Giver's Mansion

Moggallana Bhante:
Devata, your beauty shines in all directions like the bright star named Osadhi. What are the meritorious deeds that led to this happiness?

Tell me Devata, what kind of meritorious action did you do when you were in the human world to have gained this beauty that shines in all directions, and to have earned all these wonderful things?

That devata, delighted at being questioned by Arahant Moggallana, gladly explained what she had done that resulted in such great happiness.

Devata:

Bhante, before I was born here, I lived in the human world. One day, I saw the Supreme Buddha who had a happy, pure, and calm mind. I happily offered alms to the Buddha with my own hands.

Because of this meritorious deed, I have been born as a very beautiful devata and enjoy all the wonderful things that delight my heart.

Great Bhante, that was the meritorious action I did to have such a beautiful body that shines in all directions.

2.11 Second Alms Giver's Mansion

Moggallana Bhante:

Devata, your beauty shines in all directions like the bright star named Osadhi.

What are the meritorious deeds that led to this happiness?

Tell me Devata, what kind of meritorious action did you do when you were in the human world to have gained this beauty that shines in all directions, and to have earned all these wonderful things?

That devata, delighted at being questioned by Arahant Moggallana, gladly explained what she had done that resulted in such great happiness.

Devata:

Bhante, before I was born here, I lived in the human world. One day, I saw an Arahant monk who had a happy, pure, and calm mind. I happily offered alms to that Arahant monk with my own hands.

Because of this meritorious deed, I have been born as a very beautiful devata and enjoy all the wonderful things that delight my heart.

Great Bhante, that was the meritorious action I did to have such a beautiful body that shines in all directions.

3. The Coral Tree Chapter

3.1 Splendid Mansion

Moggallana Bhante:

Devata, you are very mighty and your beauty illuminates all the directions. Many gods and goddesses decorated with divine jewelry dance and sing to entertain you. You are superior to all of them in status and happiness. Your mansion is very beautiful. It is made of gold. You spend your time here very happily.

What kind of merit did you do to receive this result?

Tell me Devata, what kind of meritorious action did you do when you were in the human world to have such beauty as well as all these wonderful things?

That devata, delighted at being questioned by Arahant Moggallana, gladly explained what she had done that resulted in such great happiness.

Devata:

Before I was born here, I lived in the human world. I was a daughter-in-law in a very greedy family that did not have any faith in the Triple Gem. But I had unshakable confidence in the Triple Gem and I followed the Five Precepts. I delighted in giving and sharing. One day, Bhante, you came on your almsround and I offered you an oil cake.

When my mother-in-law came home, I told her, "Mother, today a monk came here. I was happy and offered an oil cake with my own hands." My mother-in-law scolded me saying, "You are a disobedient and evil girl. You did not get permission from me to give an oil cake to a monk."

She got very angry and hit me with a grinding stone, breaking my shoulder. My injury was very serious and I did not live long after that. After death, I escaped from suffering in the human world and was born among devas in Tavatimsa Heaven.

Because of this meritorious deed, I have been born as a very beautiful goddess and enjoy all the wonderful things that delight my heart.

Great Bhante, that was the meritorious action I did to have such a beautiful body that shines in all directions.

3.2 Sugar-Cane Mansion

Moggallana Bhante:
Devata, you shine like the sun which illuminates the sky and the earth. You shine like a great Brahma who shines brighter than Sakka and the Tavatimsa devas. You surpass others with your beauty, fame, and power.

Devata, you wear blue lotus garlands, your skin is the color of gold, and you wear beautiful dresses. Now that you are worshiping me, I ask you, who are you?

What kind of meritorious action did you do in the past? Did you practice generosity well, or follow the precepts? How have you been born in this heaven? What action have you done to earn this result?

Devata:
Bhante, in this same village which we are in right now, you came to our house on your almsround. I was pleased

to see you. I offered you a small piece of sugar-cane with a delighted heart.

Later, when my mother-in-law came home, she asked me, "Daughter-in-law, where did you put my sugar-cane?" I told her, "I neither threw it away nor ate it. I offered it to a peaceful monk." My mother-in-law got very angry. Scolding me she said, "Hey! Are you the owner of this house or am I? Who makes the decisions here?" She hit me with a chair and I died instantly. I was reborn as a devata in this heaven.

That was the meritorious action I did. This is how I enjoy this divine happiness surrounded by gods. The god Sakka protects the Tavatimsa Heaven and the Tavatimsa devas protect me. The result of the offering of a small piece of sugar-cane was not small. It generated great fruit. I enjoy happiness in the heavenly Nandana Park like the god Sakka.

Bhante, you are very compassionate and wise. I came here to ask about your well-being and worship you. I have received all these wonderful things having offered a small piece of sugar-cane to you willingly and with a very happy mind.

3.3 Couch Mansion

Moggallana Bhante:
Devata, you are sitting on a very comfortable couch decorated with many jewels and gold and covered with flowers. While resting here you demonstrate your wide range of psychic powers.

You are surrounded by many other goddesses who are singing, dancing and entertaining you. You are very powerful. What good deed did you do in your previous human life? What is the reason that you are very beautiful and shine in all directions?

Devata:
Bhante, in the human world I was a daughter-in-law in a very wealthy family. I never got angry at my husband and was very obedient to him. I was dedicated to practicing the Dhamma and observed the Eight Precepts happily four times a month on each of the four moon phases.

From a very young age, I was an honest wife. I tried to please my husband by day and by night. I started following the precepts when I was very young.

I abstained from killing beings, stealing, using intoxicants, and lying. My bodily conduct was very pure. I protected my celibate life well. I practiced virtue in an unbreakable way.

I observed the Eight Precepts four times a month on each of the four moon phases and protected them happily. Observance of the Eight Precepts four times a month brings great happiness to the mind.

I followed the Noble Eightfold Path which brings happy results. I was also obedient to my husband and acted in a pleasing way. I was a disciple of the Supreme Buddha from an early age.

These were the meritorious deeds I did when I lived in the human world. These specific deeds led me to a rebirth in heaven. Now I am very powerful here. This delightful mansion is very beautiful. Many beautiful goddesses entertain me. I have been born in an excellent heaven where gods have long lifespans.

3.4 Lata's Mansion

The famous god Sakka and the god Vessavana have beautiful daughters named Lata, Sajja, Pavara, Acchimukhi, and Suta. They shine due to their good qualities.

One day, these five daughters went to a magnificent river near the Himalayan Mountains to bathe. The water of the river was very cool and full of blue lotuses. These goddesses bathed in that river and sang and danced.

Goddess Suta:
Dear Lata, your skin is the color of gold, you are wearing lotus garlands decorated with golden flowers, and you have beautiful copper colored eyes. You are as beautiful as the clear sky. You will also live here for a very long time.

Please tell us, dear Lata, what kind of meritorious actions did you do in your past life to get all these wonderful things?

Fortunate sister, how were you so pleasing to your husband? Your beauty is magnificent. You are a very talented dancer and singer. Many gods and goddesses are eager to know your past meritorious deeds.

Goddess Lata:
In my previous life, I lived in the human world. I was a daughter-in-law in a very rich family. I was very obedient to my husband and never got angry at him. I was dedicated in observing the Eight Precepts. I was an honest and virtuous wife from a young age. I always made my husband happy and I tried my best to help my parents-in-law, my brother-in-law, and the servants. That is how I collected merit.

Due to those wholesome actions, I have received great divine long life, beauty, happiness, and strength. I live very happily enjoying divine entertainment.

Goddess Suta:
Sisters, haven't you heard about these meritorious deeds that Lata described? She explained it to us very well. Being virtuous wives we certainly know the value of husbands. We treated our husbands like gods. Since we respected our husbands, we were able to be loyal wives to them as Lata did. Those were the meritorious lives we lived which led us to this heaven.

A brave lion that lives in a mountain forest hunts weak animals and eats their flesh. So too, if a wife leads a virtuous life as a devoted disciple of the Buddha, is loyal to her husband, and controls her anger and greed, then such a wife enjoys a heavenly rebirth.

3.5 Guttila's Mansion

The music teacher Guttila had an arrogant student who challenged him to a competition. Guttila called on the god Sakka for assistance.

Teacher Guttila:
God Sakka, I was the one who taught my pupil Musila how to play sweet music on the guitar. But now my student has challenged me in a guitar competition. Please, Sakka, help me.

God Sakka:
Yes, certainly I will help you. I always honor teachers. The pupil will not defeat you. Teacher, you will defeat the pupil.

Upon seeing the goddesses who had come along with the god Sakka, Guttila questioned them. In the time of the Supreme Buddha, Moggallana Bhante asked them the very same questions,

Moggallana Bhante:
Devata, your beauty shines in all directions like the bright star named Osadhi.

What are the meritorious deeds that led to this happiness?

Tell me Devata, what kind of meritorious action did you do when you were in the human world to have gained this beauty that shines in all directions, and to have earned all these wonderful things?

That devata, delighted at being questioned by Moggallana Bhante, gladly explained what she had done that resulted in such great happiness.

Devata:
A woman who offers clothes is the best among men and women. In this way, the one who gives pleasing things is reborn in heaven and receives divine happiness that delights the heart.

Look at my divine mansion. I am a powerful goddess. I can change my appearance into any form I wish. I am the best of a thousand goddesses. Imagine the result of my meritorious deed.

Because of this meritorious deed, I have been born as a very beautiful devata and enjoy all the wonderful things that delight my heart.

Great Bhante, that was the meritorious action I did to have such a beautiful body that shines in all directions.

A group of devatas, one by one, answered the same question as follows:

A woman who offers flowers is the best among men and women. In this way, the one who gives pleasing things, is reborn in heaven and receives divine happiness that delights the heart.

A woman who offers perfumes is the best among men and women. In this way, the one who gives pleasing things, is reborn in heaven and receives divine happiness that delights the heart.

A woman who offers fruit is the best among men and women. In this way, the one who gives pleasing things, is reborn in heaven and receives divine happiness that delights the heart.

A woman who offers delicious foods is the best among men and women. In this way, the one who gives pleasing things, is reborn in heaven and receives divine happiness that delights the heart.

I offered five kinds of fragrances to the stupa that held the relics of Kassapa Buddha...

When I saw monks and nuns traveling along the road, I listened to the Dhamma from them and I observed Eight Precepts just for one day...

While I was standing in water, I happily offered water to a monk...

My mother-in-law and father-in-law were harsh, rough, and easily got angry, but I did not hate them nor did I say bad words to them, I treated them well and I followed Eight Precepts diligently...

I worked for others as a servant girl. I was not lazy and worked hard. I was not arrogant and did not hate others. I was happy to share whatever I had with others...

I offered milk-rice to a monk who was going on almsround. Having done similar meritorious deeds, now I enjoy heavenly happiness...

I offered a piece of golden sugar...

I offered a small piece of sugarcane...

I offered some timbaru fruit...

I offered some sweet cucumber...

I offered some cucumber...

I offered some creeper fruits...

I offered some pharusaka flowers...

I offered a pan for burning coals...

I offered a handful of vegetables...

I offered a handful of small flowers...

I offered a bundle of lotus roots...

I offered a handful of nimb leaves...

I offered some sour gruel...

I offered an oil-seed cake...

I offered a waistband...

I offered a shoulder-strap...

I offered a bandage...

I offered a fan...

I offered a palm-leaf fan...

I offered a peacock-feather fly-whisk…

I offered an umbrella…

I offered a pair of sandals…

I offered an oil-cake...

I offered a sweetmeat...

Moggallana Bhante:
Devata, your beauty shines in all directions like the bright star named Osadhi.

What are the meritorious deeds that led to this happiness?

Tell me Devata, what kind of meritorious action did you do when you were in the human world to have gained this beauty that shines in all directions, and to have earned all these wonderful things?

That devata, delighted at being questioned by Arahant Moggallana, gladly explained what she had done that resulted in such great happiness.

Devata:
I gave sweet cake to a monk who was on his almsround. Having done similar meritorious deeds, now I enjoy heavenly happiness.

Look at my divine mansion, I am a powerful goddess. I can change my appearance into any form I wish. I am the best of a thousand goddesses. Imagine the result of my meritorious deed.

Because of this meritorious deeds, I have been born as a very beautiful devata and enjoy all the wonderful things that delight my heart.

Great Bhante, those were the meritorious deeds I did to have such a beautiful body which shines in all directions.

Teacher Guttila:

It is wonderful indeed, that I have come here today. This day has started pleasantly. I have seen beautiful goddesses who are able to change their appearance as they wish.

I learned the Dhamma from them. I will do lots of meritorious deeds by giving, keeping the precepts, and restraining myself. If I do this, one day I too will be born in heaven where there is no sadness.

3.6 Dazzling Mansion

Devata Bhadda:

Devata, you are dazzling and shining in beauty, surrounded by many goddesses. You surpass all the other Tavatimsa devas in beauty.

I have not seen you before. This is the first time I have seen you. From which heaven did you come? You called me by name.

Devata Subhadda:

Dear sister, in my previous life when I was in the human world, my name was Subhadda. I was your younger sister and was a co-wife with you. After death, I departed the human world and was reborn among the devas in the Nimmanarati Heaven.

Devata Bhadda:

Those who have collected much merit are reborn in Nimmanarati Heaven. So you too have been born in this wonderful heaven, haven't you? Famous devata, who taught you to collect merit? What kind of offering did you make? What kind of precepts did you follow? We ask you, how did you gain all these wonderful things? Please tell us what meritorious deed this is the result of.

Devata Subhadda:

In my previous life when I was in the human world, I had confidence in the community of monks. They were worthy of offerings, so I offered food to eight monks with my own hands.

Because of this meritorious deed, I have been born as a very beautiful devata and enjoy all the wonderful things that delight my heart.

Sister, that was the meritorious action I did to have such a beautiful body which shines in all directions.

Devata Bhadda:

My mind also had confidence in those monks. But I offered them much more food than you did. Yet, I have been born in a lower heavenly world than you. Having offered very little, how did you receive more happiness than me? Of what meritorious deed is this the result?

Devata Subhadda:

I knew a noble monk named Revata and was inspired by him. One day I invited eight monks along with Revata Bhante, with the intention of making individual offerings. Out of compassion for me, and to help me gain more merit, Revata Bhante told me not to make individual offerings but to make an offering to the Noble Sangha, the whole community of monks. I did exactly as he advised.

My offering was made to the Noble Sangha which has immeasurable virtues. But since you offered food to individual monks, your offering was not as fruitful.

Devata Bhadda:

Oh, only now do I know that offering to the Noble Sangha as a whole bears greater fruit. When I go back to the human world, I will make offerings to the Noble Sangha and I will look after the Noble Sangha well. Letting go of greed, I will collect merit diligently.

God Sakka:

Devata Bhadda, who is this devata that you are speaking with? Her beauty surpasses all other devas in the Tavatimsa Heaven.

Devata Bhadda:

God Sakka, Leader of the Devas, in my previous human life she was my younger sister. We were co-wives of the same husband. She has offered food to the Noble Sangha and collected vast amounts of merit. That is why she shines so brilliantly.

God Sakka:

Oh Devata Bhadda, your younger sister has offered food to the Noble Sangha and as a result she shines so brilliantly.

One day, the Supreme Buddha was staying on the mountain named Vulture's Peak. I asked the Blessed One to whom should one offer food to get the greatest benefits? The Supreme Buddha had an excellent knowledge of actions and their results. The Blessed One answered, "If one wants to gain the most merit and be reborn in heaven, they should make offerings to the Noble Sangha. There are four types of disciples practicing the Path and four other types who have achieved the fruits of the Path. They are virtuous, mindful, and wise."

Devata, I know very well that this Noble Sangha has immeasurable virtues. Their lives are full of good qualities like the great ocean. They are the disciples of the best teacher among humans. These disciples illuminate the world by spreading the Dhamma.

If someone offers food and drink to the community of the Noble Sangha that gift will bear immense results. The Knower of the World, the Buddha, praised giving and encouraged people to give offerings to the Noble Sangha.

Once offerings are made to the Noble Sangha, the givers should recollect that gift and then they will have delighted hearts. They will live rejoicing in their generous nature. As a result, they will be able to be born in a wonderful heaven.

3.7 Sesavati's Mansion

Vangisa Bhante:
Dear Devata, your mansion is very beautiful. Silver and golden nets dangle from walls made of crystal. There are beautifully decorated archways and golden sand spread throughout the compound. When the sun shines in autumn, darkness is dispelled in all directions and the sky blazes. Such is your mansion. It glows just like a fire blazing in the night sky. It blinds the eye as though it were lightning. Music from guitars and drums, and clapping hands echo throughout your mansion, just like in Inda's city, which is full of entertainment. Your mansion is surrounded by jasmine flowers and red, white, and blue lotuses. Trees with blossoming sala and asoka flowers spread sweet fragrance all around.

Beautiful Devata, delightful pools surround your mansion. Their water is like blue gems. On the banks of those pools, there are beautiful sweetly scented trees and blossoming vines overhanging palm trees. All types of flowers that grow in water and trees that grow on land, both in the human and the heavenly world, can be found around your mansion.

When you were in the human world, what precepts did you follow to get this result? How did you receive this divine mansion with wonderful pleasures?

Devata:

Around my mansion live various types of divine birds such as herons, peacocks, partridges, ducks, geese, and cuckoos. Their songs can be heard all around. My mansion is surrounded by many types of divine trees and flowers such as trumpet flowers, rose-apple, and asoka trees. It is very beautiful. I will explain how I have obtained it.

Bhante, when I was in the human world, I lived in a village called Nalaka which is in the eastern part of Magadha province. I was a daughter-in-law there. My name was Sesavati.

The Arahant Sariputta Bhante attained final Nibbana at passing away. He possessed immeasurable good qualities. He was honored and respected by gods and men. He was very skilled at analyzing and explaining the Dhamma. I was also very pleased with that quality. I offered fragrant flowers to his sacred body.

He was in his final life and bearing his final body. He was a great seer. That great Bhante attained final Nibbana at passing away without leaving anything in this world.

I offered sweet-smelling flowers to his body during his funeral. Due to that meritorious deed, after death I was reborn in this Tavatimsa Heaven.

3.8 Mallika's Mansion

Narada Bhante:

Devata, you are dressed in divine golden clothes and gold jewelry. Golden banners are waving in the sky. Even without this jewelry, your beauty shines brightly. You are wearing gold bangles, bracelets, and a necklace of gems. You wear a gold crown on your head and your body is covered with a golden net.

You are decorated with various types of garlands made from gold, rubies, pearls, beryl and cat's-eye jewels. These garlands produce sweet music like the songs of peacocks, geese, and cuckoos. Your divine chariot is also decorated with beautiful gems and the color of each part on the chariot is well matched.

Your beauty shines in all directions when you travel in this chariot. Devata, what kind of meritorious actions did you do to receive this result?

Devata:

When I was in the human world, I learned about the death of Gautama Supreme Buddha who possessed immeasurable good qualities. With a very happy mind, I made a golden net and decorated it with jewels, gold, and pearls. Then I offered it to the Supreme Buddha.

In this way, I collected much merit as encouraged by the Buddha. That is how I was reborn in heaven and now enjoy happiness without any sorrow.

3.9 Mansion of the Beautiful-Eyed Goddess

God Sakka:

Devata, with large beautiful eyes you walk around surrounded by many other goddesses in the delightful Cittalata Forest. What is your name?

When the gods of the Tavatimsa Heaven enter this forest their bodies, horses, and chariots become more beautiful.

Even though you are not wearing any golden flower jewelry, you are still extremely beautiful. Tell us, what meritorious deed have you done to gain this beauty?

Devata:

Lord of Devas, I have received this heavenly birth, beautiful body, and divine psychic powers due to my meritorious deeds. I will tell you what I did.

In the human world, I lived in the beautiful city of Rajagaha. My name was Sunanda and I was a female lay disciple of the Supreme Buddha. I had faith, virtue and was very generous. I had great confidence in the noble monks with pure minds. I offered them robes, food, resting places, and lamps.

I was eager to observe the Eight Precepts four times a month on each of the four moon phases. I led a restrained life and delighted in sharing.

I abstained from killing, stealing, lying, and taking intoxicants. I did not cheat on my husband. I was delighted to keep these Five Precepts every day. I was a lay follower of Gautama Supreme Buddha who had the great wisdom to see the reality of the world. I was wise enough to realize the Four Noble Truths.

A servant girl, working for my relatives, used to bring me flower garlands every day. I offered all those flower garlands with a happy mind to the relic stupa of the Supreme Buddha. I also went to relic puja ceremonies every Eight Precepts-Observance day. With great faith, I personally offered garlands, perfumes, and ointments to the stupa. God Sakka, I received this heavenly birth, beautiful body, and divine psychic powers by offering flower garlands.

I also collected merit by keeping the precepts, but that merit has not yet ripened. Lord Sakka, in my mind I have the desire to be a once-returner.

3.10 Coral Tree Mansion

Moggallana Bhante:
Devata, this coral tree is beautiful and delightful. You are making garlands from the flowers of that tree while singing happily. When you dance, beautiful divine sounds and fragrance spread from your limbs. As you dance and as your hair waves, the bells on your hair play beautiful music. Also, as wind blows on the garland-crown on your head it plays beautiful music. Your garland-crown looks and smells very beautiful like a manjusaka tree full of fragrant flowers.

Do you smell these scents? Have you seen your beauty? We now ask you, what kind of meritorious actions did you do to have gained these results?

Devata:
When I was in the human world, one day I made a garland out of asoka flowers. It was so pretty and smelled delightful. I offered that flower garland to the Supreme Buddha.

In this way, I practiced lots of meritorious deeds as encouraged by the Buddha. This is why today I live very happily in this heaven without any sorrow or pain.

4. The Crimson Chapter

4.1 Crimson Mansion

Moggallana Bhante:
Dear Devata, your mansion is crimson colored. Golden sand spreads all over your compound. Delightful music is always playing. You enjoy listening to that music very much.

Now you leave your mansion made of gems and walk towards the park of sala trees, full of beautiful flowers. When you go under a sala tree, something wonderful happens: the branches of the tree bend towards you and shower you with flowers. There are many beautiful birds in the park. Sala trees are blown by the wind in a beautiful rhythm, spreading their fragrance in all directions.

Do you smell these scents? Have you seen your beauty? We now ask you, what kind of meritorious actions did you do to gain these results?

Devata:
In my previous life I lived in the human world. I was a servant girl in a good family. One day, the Supreme Buddha visited my master's house. I was very happy to see the Buddha sitting inside the house. I offered sala flowers spreading them around the Blessed One. I also made a beautiful garland-crown out of sala flowers and with delight offered it to the Supreme Buddha.

In this way, I practiced lots of meritorious deeds as encouraged by the Buddha. This is why today I live very happily in this heaven without any sorrow or pain.

4.2 Shining Mansion

Moggallana Bhante:

Devata, you shine brilliantly and colorfully. You are dressed in divine red clothing. Your body is as beautiful as if you had applied sandalwood cream. You seem to be very mighty, possessing psychic powers. Now you are worshiping me. Who are you?

Your throne is also valuable and decorated with various types of gems. When you are sitting on it, you shine like Sakka, King of Gods, in the heavenly Nandana Park.

Beautiful Devata, what kind of virtuous life did you lead in the past? We now ask you, what kind of meritorious actions did you do to gain these results?

Devata:

Bhante, when I was in the human world, one day while you were going on your almsround, I offered a flower garland and a piece of golden sugar to you. As a result of that meritorious deed, I enjoy this happiness today.

But Bhante, I feel very regretful because of a mistake I made. I did not listen to the excellent teachings preached by the King of Dhamma, the Supreme Buddha.

Bhante, please listen to me. If anybody has compassion for me they should encourage me to practice that excellent teaching of the Supreme Buddha.

Those devas who possess strong confidence in the Supreme Buddha, the Supreme Dhamma, and the Supreme Sangha outshine me in heavenly life span, fame, and radiance. Those other devas are very beautiful, mighty, and powerful. They experience much more happiness than I do.

4.3 Elephant Mansion

Vangisa Bhante:

Devata, you are traveling in the sky on the back of a very large divine elephant who has psychic powers. Your elephant is decorated with a beautiful golden net and golden flowers. On the elephant's two tusks, there are beautiful ponds with crystal clear water and many lotus flowers. In the middle of each lotus, a devata is dancing to divine music.

Devata, you are very powerful even amongst the gods, shining brightly in all directions. what kind of meritorious actions did you do when you were in the human world?

Devata:

When I was in the human world, one day I went to Baranasi to see the Supreme Buddha. I offered a pair of robes to the Blessed One, worshiped his sacred feet, and sat down and paid homage to the Buddha by happily placing my hands together.

The Supreme Buddha's body shines with the color of pure gold. The Great Teacher taught me the cause of suffering, the suffering of this impermanent life, the unconditioned sorrowless state, the supreme bliss of Nibbana, and the Noble Eightfold Path which leads to the destruction of defilements.

My lifespan was very short. After death I was reborn among the devas of the Tavatimsa Heaven where there is much entertainment. Now I am a wife of the god Sakka. My name is Yasuttara and everybody knows who I am.

4.4 Aloma's Mansion

Moggallana Bhante:
Devata, your beauty shines in all directions like the bright star named Osadhi.

What are the meritorious deeds that led to this happiness?

Tell me Devata, what kind of meritorious action did you do when you were in the human world to have gained this beauty that shines in all directions, and to have earned all these wonderful things?

That devata, delighted at being questioned by Arahant Moggallana, gladly explained what she had done that resulted in such great happiness.

Devata:
In the human world I lived in the city of Baranasi. The Supreme Buddha was born in the Clan of the Sun. Therefore he is known as the Kinsman of the Sun. One day I happily offered a dry lump of rice cake to the Supreme Buddha.

The lump of rice cake I gave was very dry, unsalted and not tasty. But look at the result of that tiny offering! When others see how I enjoy life here, who would not want to collect merit?

Because of this meritorious deed, I have been born as a very beautiful devata and enjoy all the wonderful things that delight my heart.

Great Bhante, that was the meritorious action I did to have such a beautiful body that shines in all directions.

4.5 Rice-Gruel-Giver's Mansion

Moggallana Bhante:

Devata, your beauty shines in all directions like the bright star named Osadhi.

What are the meritorious deeds that led to this happiness?

Tell me Devata, what kind of meritorious action did you do when you were in the human world to have gained this beauty that shines in all directions, and to have earned all these wonderful things?

That devata, delighted at being questioned by Arahant Moggallana, gladly explained what she had done that resulted in such great happiness.

Devata:

In the human world I lived in the city of Andhakavinda. One day I offered some gruel cooked with jujube and flavored with oil to the Supreme Buddha, Kinsman of the Sun. I tried to make it very delicious adding pepper, garlic, and other tasty ingredients. With a delighted heart I offered that medicinal gruel to the Supreme Buddha.

If one becomes the beautiful queen on a wheel-turning monarch, the happiness she experiences is not even worth a sixteenth part of the result of this rice-gruel gift.

A hundred gold coins, a hundred horses, a hundred chariots pulled by mules, a hundred thousand maidens decorated in beautiful ornaments—happiness gained from these items is not worth a sixteenth part of the result of this rice-gruel gift.

Even the happiness gained from a hundred Himalayan elephants with round tusks like wheels and necks decorated with golden ornaments is not worth a sixteenth part of the result of this rice-gruel gift.

Even if someone became the ruler of this whole earth, a wheel-turning monarch, even his happiness is not worth a sixteenth part of the result of this rice-gruel gift.

4.6 Monastery Mansion

Anuruddha Bhante:
Devata, your beauty shines in all directions like the bright star named Osadhi.

When you dance, beautiful divine sounds and fragrance come from your limbs. As you dance and as your hair blows, the bells in your hair play lovely music. Also, as wind blows on the garland-crown on your head it plays sweet music. Your garland-crown looks and smells beautiful like a manjusaka tree full of fragrant flowers.

Do you smell these scents? Have you seen your beauty? We now ask you, what kind of meritorious actions did you do to have gained these results?

Devata:
Bhante, in the human world I had a friend who lived in the city of Savatthi. She built a great monastery for the community of monks. I was extremely happy about that. I sincerely rejoiced in her gift and the merit that she gained. The sight of that monastery was pleasing to my eyes.

As a result of truly rejoicing in my friend's meritorious deed, this wonderful divine mansion has appeared for me.

Due to the power of my meritorious deed, this divine mansion spreads for sixteen kilometers into the sky and shines brightly in all directions. In my mansion, there are huge rooms divided into sections.

There are lotus ponds filled with heavenly fish. The water in the pond is clear, filled with many kinds of lotuses that give off a sweet smell when the wind blows. The banks of the pond are covered with golden sand.

Inside my mansion grow all sorts of trees: rose-apples, jackfruits, palms and coconuts. I am surrounded by beautiful music and the sound of many goddesses. Even if someone sees me only in a dream they will be happy.

A mansion like mine, excellent, beautiful and gleaming, has been created for me because of my meritorious deeds. This is why we should do good actions.

Anuruddha Bhante:
Since you rejoiced in your friend's excellent gift, you have received this beautiful mansion. Tell me what happened to your friend. Where was she reborn?

Devata:
That friend of mine offered that large monastery for the Noble Sangha. She understood the Four Noble Truths clearly and made offerings with that understanding. She was reborn in the Nimmanarati Heaven. She is now the chief queen of Sunimmita, king of that heaven. I can't even imagine the sensual pleasures she is now enjoying because of her gift. You asked me where she was reborn, and I told you as it is.

After hearing about the results of this gift, tell others to happily give gifts to the Noble Sangha and listen to the

Dhamma with minds of faith. To be born as a human is very rare, and now you have this chance.

The Supreme Buddha, with golden skin and a sweet voice, taught us this excellent way: happily give gifts to the Noble Sangha, where gifts give the best results.

The Noble Sangha has eight kinds of people grouped in four pairs. These disciples of the Buddha are worthy of gifts. Gifts given to them will be of great fruit: Stream-Enterer, Once-Returner, Non-Returner, Arahant, and the other four who are on the path to these states. The Noble Sangha is true to their purpose with concentration, wisdom, and morality.

Human beings give alms wanting to make merit. The merit they gain when giving to the Noble Sangha will bear fruitful results in their future lives.

The Noble Sangha is full of goodness and has become great. It is impossible to measure its greatness, just as it is impossible to measure the water in the ocean. Followers of the Great Hero, the Supreme Buddha, are the best kind of people, bringing light wherever they preach the Dhamma.

Those who give gifts such as food, shelter, medicine, and clothing to the whole Noble Sangha, have given their gifts correctly, have made their offerings correctly, and have made their sacrifice correctly. Those gifts are very beneficial and are praised by the Supreme Buddha, the Knower of the World.

People should always recollect the gifts they have given to the Noble Sangha. This will bring them happiness. They should completely remove the stain of stinginess. Then they can be born in heaven and be praised by the wise.

4.7 Four Women Mansion

Moggallana Bhante saw four devatas and questioned each of them.

Moggallana Bhante:
Devata, your beauty shines in all directions like the bright star named Osadhi.

What are the meritorious deeds that led to this happiness?

Tell me Devata, what kind of meritorious action did you do when you were in the human world to have gained this beauty that shines in all directions, and to have earned all these wonderful things?

The first devata, delighted at being questioned by Arahant Moggallana, gladly explained what she had done that resulted in such great happiness.

First Devata:
In the human world I lived in the great city of Pannakata in the mountains of Esika. One day, I saw a monk going on his almsround and I offered him a bouquet of yellow flowers.

Because of this meritorious deed, I have been born as a very beautiful devata and enjoy all the wonderful things that delight my heart.

That is why the pure radiance of my body and limbs is stainless and shines in all directions.

Great Bhante, that is the meritorious action I did to have such a beautiful body.

Moggallana Bhante:
Devata, your beauty shines in all directions like the bright star named Osadhi.

What is the meritorious deed that led to this happiness?

Tell me Devata, what kind of meritorious action did you do when you were in the human world to have gained this beauty that shines in all directions, and to have earned all these wonderful things?

The second devata, delighted at being questioned by Arahant Moggallana, gladly explained what she had done that resulted in such great happiness.

Second Devata:
In the human world I lived in the great city of Pannakata in the mountains of Esika. One day, I saw a monk going on his almsround and I offered him a bouquet of blue water lilies.

Because of this meritorious deed, I have been born as a very beautiful devata and enjoy all the wonderful things that delight my heart.

That is why the pure radiance of my body and limbs is stainless and shines in all directions.

Great Bhante, that is the meritorious action I did to have such a beautiful body.

Moggallana Bhante:
Devata, your beauty shines in all directions like the bright star named Osadhi.

What is the meritorious deed that led to this happiness?

Tell me Devata, what kind of meritorious action did you do when you were in the human world to have gained this beauty that shines in all directions, and to have earned all these wonderful things?

The third devata, delighted at being questioned by Arahant Moggallana, gladly explained what she had done that resulted in such great happiness.

Third Devata:
In the human world I lived in the great city of Pannakata in the mountains of Esika. One day, I saw a monk going on his almsround and I gave him a bouquet of lotuses with white roots and green leaves which I picked from the pond.

Because of this meritorious deed, I have been born as a very beautiful devata and enjoy all the wonderful things that delight my heart.

That is why the pure radiance of my body and limbs is stainless and shines in all directions.

Great Bhante, that is the meritorious action I did to have such a beautiful body.

Moggallana Bhante:
Devata, your beauty shines in all directions like the bright star named Osadhi.

What is the meritorious deed that led to this happiness?

Tell me Devata, what kind of meritorious action did you do when you were in the human world to have gained this beauty that shines in all directions, and to have earned all these wonderful things?

The fourth devata, delighted at being questioned by Arahant Moggallana, gladly explained what she had done that resulted in such great happiness.

Fourth Devata:
In the human world I lived in the great city of Pannakata in the mountains of Esika. One day, I saw a monk going

on his almsround and I gave him a bouquet of ivory colored jasmine buds.

Because of this meritorious deed, I have been born as a very beautiful devata and enjoy all the wonderful things that delight my heart.

That is why the pure radiance of my body and limbs is stainless and shines in all directions.

Great Bhante, that is the meritorious action I did to have such a beautiful body.

4.8 Mango Mansion

Moggallana Bhante:
Dear Devata, your heavenly mango grove is delightful and your mansion is very large. The sound of various musical instruments and the chatting of happy devatas can be heard around the mansion. There is a golden lamp that never goes out. There are trees with fruits made of divine cloth.

What are the meritorious deeds that led to this happiness?

Tell me Devata, what kind of meritorious action did you do when you were in the human world to have gained this beauty that shines in all directions, and to have earned all these wonderful things?

That devata, delighted at being questioned by Arahant Moggallana, gladly explained what she had done that resulted in such great happiness.

Devata:
In my previous life, I was a woman in the human world. I built a monastery and offered it to the Noble Sangha. That monastery was surrounded by mango trees. When

the monastery was completed, at the opening ceremony, I decorated the trees with ornaments shaped like mangoes that I made from beautiful cloth. I lit a lamp there and offered alms to the monks. On that day, with a happy mind, I offered that monastery to the Noble Sangha with my own hands.

That is why I have received this delightful heavenly mango grove and large mansion. The sound of various musical instruments and the chatting of happy devatas can be heard around the mansion. There is a golden lamp that never goes out. There are trees with fruits made of divine cloth.

Because of these meritorious deeds, I have been born as a very beautiful devata and enjoy all the wonderful things that delight my heart.

That is why the pure radiance of my body and limbs is stainless and shines in all directions.

Great Bhante, those were the meritorious deeds I did to have such a beautiful body.

4.9 Mansion of Yellow Flowers

God Sakka:
Dear Deva, you are wearing yellow clothes and jewelry. You have put on yellow sandalwood cream and you have decorated yourself with yellow lotuses and yellow scarves. Your mansion is yellow; even your furniture is yellow. Furthermore, your plates and bowls are yellow. There are also yellow umbrellas, vehicles, horses, and fans. Everything in this mansion is yellow.

Tell me Devata, what kind of meritorious action did you do when you were in the human world? We ask about the action that gave this result.

Devata:
God Sakka, Lord of Devas, in the human world there were vines with tiny yellow flowers. One day I plucked four flowers without thinking about gaining any special results. Then I went to the stupa containing the relics of the Supreme Buddha.

While I was thinking about the sacred body of the Supreme Buddha, my heart was delighted. I was always thinking about that stupa. I did not realize there was a cow chasing me.

Before I could offer the flowers to the stupa, I was killed by that cow. If I had collected the merit of offering the flowers, my happiness would have been much better than this. Great Sakka, because of that meritorious deed, I was reborn here after I left the human world.

The leader of the Tavatimsa Heaven, God Sakka, also called Maghava, told his chariot driver, Deva Matali, about that excellent meritorious deed. Other devas were also happily listening to him.

God Sakka:
Dear Matali, look at this excellent result. Isn't this wonderful? Although the object which she was going to offer was very small, it generated a great result. If one gives even a very small thing with a confident heart to the Supreme Buddha or to a disciple of the Buddha, the result is not small.

Dear Matali, come, we too shall go worship the relics of the Supreme Buddha. Collecting merit always gives happiness. If people offer something to the Supreme Buddha when he is alive or after he has passed away, as long as they have the same confident mind on both occasions, the results will be the same. Beings are reborn in heaven because of their confident minds.

Those who respect the Supreme Buddha are reborn in heaven. Surely, Supreme Buddhas are born into this world for the benefit of all beings.

4.10 Sugar Cane Mansion

Moggallana Bhante:
Devata, you shine like the sun which illuminates the sky and the earth. You shine like a great Brahma who shines brighter than Sakka and the Tavatimsa devas. You surpass others with your beauty, fame, and power.

Devata, you are wearing blue lotus garlands, your skin is the color of gold, and you are adorned with beautiful gowns. Now that you are worshiping me, I ask you: who are you?

What kind of meritorious action did you do in the past? Did you practice generosity well, or follow precepts? How were you born in this heaven? I ask you about the action that gave this result.

Devata:
Bhante, in this village where we are now, you came to our house on your almsround. I was pleased to see you. I offered you a small piece of sugar-cane with a delighted heart.

Later, when my mother-in-law came home, she asked me, "Daughter-in-law, where did you put my sugar-cane?" and I told her, "I neither threw it away nor ate it.

I offered it to a peaceful monk." My mother-in-law got very angry. Scolding me, she said, "Hey! Are you the owner of this house or am I? Who makes the decisions here?" She hit me with a stone and I died instantly. I was reborn as a devata in this heaven.

That was the meritorious action I did to enjoy this divine happiness surrounded by gods. The god Sakka protects the Tavatimsa Heaven and the Tavatimsa devas protect me. The result of the offering of a small sugar-cane was not small. It bore great fruit. I enjoy happiness in the heavenly Nandana Park like the god Sakka.

Bhante, you are very compassionate and wise. I came here to ask about your well-being and to worship you. I have received all these wonderful things having offered a small piece of sugar-cane to you with a mind of faith and a joyful heart.

4.11 Honoring Mansion

Moggallana Bhante:
Devata, your beauty shines in all directions like the bright star named Osadhi.

What are the meritorious deeds that led to this happiness?

Tell me Devata, what kind of meritorious action did you do when you were in the human world to have gained this beauty that shines in all directions, and to have earned all these wonderful things?

That devata, delighted at being questioned by Arahant Moggallana, gladly explained what she had done that resulted in such great happiness.

Devata:

Previously, I was a woman in the human world. I saw many virtuous monks and worshiped their feet with a very happy mind. I worshiped and honored them by putting my hands together.

Because of this meritorious deed, I have been born as a very beautiful devata and enjoy all the wonderful things that delight my heart.

That is why the pure radiance of my body and limbs is stainless and shines in all directions.

Great Bhante, that is the meritorious action I did to have such a beautiful body.

4.12 Rajjumala's Mansion

Moggallana Bhante:

Devata, your beauty shines in all directions like the bright star named Osadhi.

When you dance, divine music and sweet fragrance spread from your hands and feet. Also, the ornaments on your head play delightful music. The bouquet of flowers on your head spreads sweet fragrance, like that of a manjusaka tree, and plays music when the breeze blows on it. Surely, you must smell that fragrance and see your own divine body?

Tell me Devata, what kind of meritorious action did you do when you were in the human world to have gained this beauty that shines in all directions, and to have earned all these wonderful things?

Devata:

In my previous life, I was in the human world living in the city called Gaya. I was a servant girl working in a high-caste family. I did not have much merit and was very unfortunate. Everybody called me Rajjumala. I was abused, threatened, and beaten. I was tired of living that way.

One day I took a water pot and, pretending to get some water, I ran away. I ran into the forest beside the road. There I contemplated suicide. I thought that there was no point in living like this. I made a strong noose and tied it to a tree. I looked around to see whether anybody was there. Then I saw the Supreme Buddha, the most compassionate teacher of all beings in the world, sitting at the root of a tree meditating, free from all fears.

I was shocked and surprised. The hairs on my body stood on end. I thought, "Who is that being in this forest – is he a human or a god?" The sight of him was thrilling. He has escaped from the forest of defilements and attained the bliss of calmness. When I saw him I was delighted. I realized that he was not an ordinary human. The Blessed One lived with restrained senses, delighting in meditation with his mind established in Nibbana. Truly, he is the Supreme Buddha, the most compassionate teacher in the world.

Like a lion living in his cave, the Blessed One is not afraid of anything. Seeing a brave Buddha is very rare, like seeing an udumbara flower. The Supreme Buddha called to me gently, saying, "Rajjumala," and asked me to go for refuge to the Supreme Buddha. When I heard those sweet, gentle, meaningful, soft, and lovely words all my sorrows went away. My mind was joyful and clean. I was ready to understand the Dhamma. At that time, the most compassionate teacher in the world taught me the Dhamma, saying, "This is suffering, this is the cause of suffering, this is the end of suffering, and this is the way leading to deathlessness." I followed the advice of the most compassionate and skilled teacher, the Supreme Buddha. I understood the peaceful and deathless state, Nibbana. With the realization of the Four Noble Truths, my love towards the Buddha became strong, unshakable, well rooted and well established. I became a daughter born of the heart of the Supreme Buddha.

Now, I enjoy living in this heaven, playing and dancing. I do not have any fear of falling into the plains of misery again. I wear divine flower garlands and drink water from the divine river Madhumaddava. Sixty thousand musical instruments wake me from my sleep. Devas entertain me. Their names are Alamba, Gaggara, Bhima, Sadhuvadin, Samsaya, Pokkhara, and Suphassa. Other devatas, including Vina, Mokkha, Nanda, Sunanda, Sonadinna, Sucimhita, Alambusa, Missakesi, Pundarika, Athicharuni, Eniphassa, Suphassa, Subhadda, and Muduvadini entertain me as well. These and many other devatas entertain me with divine music coming to me whenever I wish. They approach me saying, "Come now! Let's dance and sing! We are here to entertain you."

Those without merit will not receive mansions like this. Only those with merit receive this happiness in the heavenly Nandana Park in the Tavatimsa Heaven.

Those who have not collected merit will not get any happiness in their current life or the next. Only those who have collected merit get happiness in both the current and next life. Those who would like to be reborn in the Tavatimsa Heaven must collect much merit. Only people who do good things are able to enjoy heavenly pleasures.

Definitely, Supreme Buddhas are born into this world for the happiness of all beings. Thus, Buddhas are the unique treasure of fields where donors can plant their seed of merit. Having respected such great beings, these fortunate people enjoy heavenly pleasures.

5. The Great Chariot Chapter

5.1 Frog-Deva's Mansion

Supreme Buddha:

Dear Deva, you are very mighty with many psychic powers. Your beautiful body shines in all directions. Now you are honoring my feet. Who are you?

Devata:

In my previous life, I was a frog living in a lake. One day I was listening to you preach. At that time a boy who was looking after cows while listening to you preach, accidentally killed me.

For just a brief moment, my mind was very pleased in hearing your voice. But now look at my psychic powers, fame, and beautiful body that I have earned from that very small act of merit.

Oh Gautama Buddha, those people who have been listening to your Dhamma for a long time will attain the fruit of the path where they escape from sorrow.

5.2 Revati's Mansion

In praise of the lay follower Nandiya's generosity, the Supreme Buddha uttered the following verse.

Supreme Buddha:

When somebody safely returns home having lived in a far away country for a long time, his relatives, friends, and associates welcome him with joy. In the same way, when someone who does meritorious acts in this world goes to the next world, his own meritorious deeds will welcome him.

Nandiya asked Revati, his wife, to continue practicing generosity when he went away, but Revati stopped. When it was time for her to die, she was addressed by two messengers from hell.

Hell Wardens:

Evil, greedy Revati! Now you must get up. The doors of hell are opening for you. Evil doers have to suffer terribly in hell. We are here to bring you to that miserable world.

Both hell wardens with big red eyes grabbed Revati's hands. They first took her to the Tavatimsa Heaven, where her husband had been reborn.

Revati:

What a wonderful mansion this is! It is made of golden nets, shining like the rays of the sun and filled with beautiful gods. Whose mansion is this? Goddesses with beautiful bodies adorned with sandalwood cream beautify the whole mansion. Who enjoys this heavenly mansion?

Hell Wardens:

In the human world, in the city of Baranasi there was a lay follower named Nandiya who was generous and helpful to others. He is the owner of this beautiful mansion. Goddesses with beautiful bodies adorned with sandalwood cream beautify the whole mansion. Nandiya enjoys this heavenly mansion.

Revati:
Ah! I was Nandiya's wife. I had authority over the whole family. I want to stay and enjoy my husband's mansion. I don't even want to see hell, let alone live there.

Hell Wardens:
Evil woman, the hell for you is down there. You did not do anything to earn merit in the human world. Those who are greedy, make others angry, and lead evil lives can never live with gods.

Revati:
Oh, what is that terrible smell? What is that rotten excrement, urine, and filth?

Hell Wardens:
Evil Revati, this is Samsavaka hell. It is as deep as the height of more than one hundred humans. You are going to boil here for a thousand years.

Revati:
Why? What bad action did I do by body, speech, and mind to have to boil in this terrible hell?

Hell Wardens:
You deceived monks, beggars, and virtuous people with lies. Those were your evil deeds. That is why you have to suffer in this deep hell for a thousand years.

In this hell, beings' hands are cut off, legs are cut off, ears are cut off, and noses are cut off. Then a flock of ravens chase the beings and eat their flesh with their sharp beaks.

Revati:
No, no! Please take me back to the human world. Surely I will do more meritorious deeds. I will practice

generosity, behave well, keep the precepts, and restrain my senses. I will do many meritorious deeds which lead to happiness and freedom from remorse.

Hell Wardens:

You are too late. You were heedless in the human world. Now weep! You will experience the results of what you did.

Revati:

Now, when I go back to the human world, who will encourage me to collect merit? Who will ask me to offer robes, shelter, food and drinks to virtuous people? Who will teach me that greedy, angry, and evil people won't go to heaven?

Surely when I go from this world to the human world I will practice generosity, behave well, keep the precepts, and restrain the senses. I will do many meritorious deeds.

I will enthusiastically make bridges in places where it is hard to cross, plant trees, set out pots of water for drinking, build parks and ponds. Furthermore, I will observe the Eight Precepts four times a month on each of the four moon phases. I will protect the precepts carefully and practice generosity eagerly. I have seen the results of merit with my own eyes.

Shaken with fear, Revati was deluded in thinking that she could return to the human world. The hell wardens grabbed her legs, turned her upside down and threw her into the terrible Samsavaka Hell.

Revati:
Previously I was very greedy and insulted monks and virtuous people. I cheated on my husband and lied to him. Now I am boiling in this frightful hell.

5.3 The Boy Chatta's Mansion

These three verses contain the qualities of the Triple Gem and were taught to a boy named Chatta by the Supreme Buddha who asked him to go for refuge.

The Sage of the Sakyan clan, the Supreme Buddha, who completed the journey to Nibbana, is the best among humans. The Blessed One crossed over Samsara with his excellent wisdom and effort. Go for refuge to this Great Teacher, the Supreme Buddha.

The Dhamma, taught by the Supreme Buddha, helps beings remove desires, craving, and sorrows. This sweet, well explained, well analyzed Dhamma is never disagreeable. Go for refuge to this great teaching, the Supreme Dhamma.

The Blessed One's noble disciples consist of the Four Pairs and the Eight Individuals. Those who offer gifts to these people gain fruitful results. Go for refuge to these excellent disciples, the Supreme Sangha.

After Chatta's death he was reborn as a deva. One day he went to see the Supreme Buddha. In order for others to learn about merit, the Supreme Buddha then questioned him in the following way.

Supreme Buddha:
Neither the sun, nor the moon, nor the star Phusa is as bright as your mansion. Your large bright mansion

shines in the sky brilliantly. What heavenly world did you come from today?

The radiance of your mansion can be seen for more than two thousand kilometers. This beautiful mansion shines both at night and day – pure, bright, and brilliant.

Around the palace there are beautiful flowers – red lotuses, white lotuses, and water lilies. Golden nets with fancy carvings are hanging there; they too shine like the sun. The mansion is decorated with divine red and yellow cloth and filled with the sweet fragrance of aloe, piyangu, and sandalwood. The mansion is surrounded by devatas with bright golden-colored bodies. It looks like the beautiful night sky covered by stars.

Devas and devatas are different colors here. Their bodies and hair are decorated with various flowers and ornaments. Golden flowers release a sweet smell when the breeze blows.

How did you receive these wonderful things? What meritorious action did you do to have gained this wonderful result? Is it because of your virtue or restrained life? Could you please explain it to me?

Devata:
One day a boy was walking on a road. You, the Great Teacher, met him and advised him by preaching the Dhamma. That boy, Chatta, promised to follow you, the Great Teacher, like a precious gem.

I was that boy, Bhante. When you asked me to go for refuge to the Buddha, the Great Victor, the Dhamma and the Noble Sangha, at first I told you that I did not know what they were. Once you had explained them to me, I went for refuge to the Triple Gem.

Wise people do not praise the actions of evil people who kill. You asked me if I knew about the precept of abstaining from killing living beings. At first I told you that I did not know about it. Once you had explained it to me, I observed that precept.

You asked me if I knew about the precept of not taking others' belongings if they are not given to us. At first I told you that I did not know about it. Once you had explained it to me, I observed that precept.

You asked me if I knew about the precept of not going to others' wives since it is a very low thing. At first I told you that I did not know about it. Once you had explained it to me, I observed that precept.

You asked me if I knew about the precept of not saying things as if they were true when I know they are not. Lying is not praised by the wise. At first I told you that I did not know about it. Once you had explained it to me, I observed that precept.

You asked me if I knew about the precept of not using intoxicants, by which one loses mindfulness. At first I told you that I did not know about it. Once you had explained it to me, I observed that precept.

On that day, I observed the Five Precepts and followed the Great Teacher's Dhamma. Later, when I reached an intersection on the road, I was surrounded by a gang of robbers. They killed me just to take my money.

Going for refuge and observing the Five Precepts is the only merit I recollect doing. I did not obtain any other merit in my life. As a result of those meritorious deeds, I was reborn in this Tavatimsa Heaven and now experience all the happiness that I wish for.

I kept those precepts for just a moment. Look at the amazing result of practicing the Dhamma! When devas with lesser pleasures than I have seen me shining brilliantly with superior pleasures, they wish to be like me.

Think about the excellence of a very brief teaching. I went to heaven and received divine happiness. If that is the case, I think those who listen to this Dhamma frequently will surely attain the state of fearlessness, the supreme bliss of Nibbana.

Even if a very small meritorious deed is practiced in this Dhamma, very great results can be expected. Look at the god Chatta who collected merit, lighting up heaven like the sun illuminating the earth.

Some gods get together and talk about me saying, "What are the meritorious deeds that he did to have gained these results? What kind of good things should be practiced? When we gain a human birth again, we will observe the Precepts and practice the Dhamma."

My great teacher helped me very much. He was compassionate towards me and came to meet me, under the hot sun. Today I have come to you again, Great Teacher. You are the truth in this world. Please be compassionate towards me. I would like to listen to the Dhamma.

When the disciples in this teaching abandon sensual desire, desire for existence, and delusion, they will never come back to sleep in the mother's womb. They attain final Nibbana at passing away and become calm.

5.4 Crab-Soup Giver's Mansion

Moggallana Bhante:
Dear Devata, your mansion is way up in the sky and spreads over one hundred and twenty kilometers. Pillars of beryl and other gemstones, and seven hundred pinnacled buildings are in your estate. It is very beautiful. Inside the mansion, you drink and eat and enjoy the sweetness of heavenly food. Guitars play sweet music. You have the five kinds of sensual pleasures. Devatas dance for you, wearing gold jewelry.

What are the meritorious deeds that led to this happiness?

Tell me Devata, what kind of meritorious action did you do when you were in the human world to have gained this beauty that shines in all directions, and to have earned all these wonderful things?

That devata, delighted at being questioned by Arahant Moggallana, gladly explained what she had done that resulted in such great happiness.

Devata:
There is a golden crab hanging on my door reminding me about my meritorious deed. It has ten legs and shines brilliantly. That is why the pure radiance of my body and limbs is stainless and shines in all directions. Great Bhante, that is the meritorious action I did to have such a beautiful body.

5.5 Doorkeeper's Mansion

Moggallana Bhante:
Dear Devata, your mansion is way up in the sky and spreads over one hundred and twenty kilometers. Pillars of beryl and other gemstones, and seven hundred

pinnacled buildings are in your estate. It is very beautiful. Inside the mansion, you drink and eat and enjoy the sweetness of heavenly food. Guitars play sweet music. You have the five kinds of sensual pleasures. Devatas dance for you, wearing gold jewelry.

What are the meritorious deeds that led to this happiness?

Tell me Devata, what kind of meritorious action did you do when you were in the human world to have gained this beauty that shines in all directions, and to have earned all these wonderful things?

That devata, delighted at being questioned by Arahant Moggallana, gladly explained what she had done that resulted in such great happiness.

Devata:
I have a lifespan of one thousand heavenly years. When I was in the human world, I spoke good words and lived with a clean and happy mind. Those were the only meritorious deeds I did. Because of that, I have gained this divine happiness.

That is why the pure radiance of my body and limbs is stainless and shines in all directions. Great Bhante, those were the meritorious deeds I did to have such a beautiful body.

5.6 Should-Be-Done Mansion

Moggallana Bhante:
Dear Devata, your mansion is way up in the sky and spreads over one hundred and twenty kilometers. Pillars of beryl and other gemstones, and seven hundred pinnacled buildings are in your estate. It is very beautiful. Inside the mansion, you drink and eat and enjoy the

sweetness of heavenly food. Guitars play sweet music. You have the five kinds of sensual pleasures. Devatas dance for you, wearing gold jewelry.

What are the meritorious deeds that led to this happiness?

Tell me Devata, what kind of meritorious action did you do when you were in the human world to have gained this beauty that shines in all directions, and to have earned all these wonderful things?

That devata, delighted at being questioned by Arahant Moggallana, gladly explained what she had done that resulted in such great happiness.

Devata:
Wise people, understanding their own well-being, should do meritorious deeds. The Supreme Buddha has completed the journey of the right path. Offerings that are given to such Buddhas generate great fruit.

Fortunately for me, one day the Supreme Buddha visited my village after coming out of a forest. My mind gained confidence in the Buddha. That is how I came to this Tavatimsa Heaven.

Because of this meritorious deed, I have been born as a very beautiful devata and enjoy all the wonderful things that delight my heart.

Great Bhante, that was the meritorious action I did to have such a beautiful body which shines in all directions.

5.7 Second Should-Be-Done Mansion

Moggallana Bhante:
Dear Devata, your mansion is way up in the sky and spreads over one hundred and twenty kilometers.

Pillars of beryl and other gemstones, and seven hundred pinnacled buildings are in your estate. It is very beautiful. Inside the mansion, you drink and eat and enjoy the sweetness of heavenly food. Guitars play sweet music. You have the five kinds of sensual pleasures. Devatas dance for you, wearing gold jewelry.

What are the meritorious deeds that led to this happiness?

Tell me Devata, what kind of meritorious action did you do when you were in the human world to have gained this beauty that shines in all directions, and to have earned all these wonderful things?

That devata, delighted at being questioned by Arahant Moggallana, gladly explained what she had done that resulted in such great happiness.

Devata:
Wise people, understanding their own well-being, should do meritorious deeds. The offering that is given to noble monks who have traveled on the correct path bears great fruit.

Fortunately for me, one day, those monks visited my village after coming out of a forest. My mind gained confidence in them. That is how I came to this Tavatimsa Heaven.

Because of this meritorious deed, I have been born as a very beautiful devata and enjoy all the wonderful things that delight my heart.

Great Bhante, that was the meritorious action I did to have such a beautiful body which shines in all directions.

5.8 Needle Mansion

Moggallana Bhante:
Dear Devata, your mansion is way up in the sky and spreads over one hundred and twenty kilometers. Pillars of beryl and other gemstones, and seven hundred pinnacled buildings are in your estate. It is very beautiful. Inside the mansion, you drink and eat and enjoy the sweetness of heavenly food. Guitars play sweet music. You have the five kinds of sensual pleasures. Devatas wearing gold jewelry dance for you.

What are the meritorious deeds that led to this happiness?

Tell me Devata, what kind of meritorious action did you do when you were in the human world to have gained this beauty that shines in all directions, and to have earned all these wonderful things?

That devata, delighted at being questioned by Arahant Moggallana, gladly explained what she had done that resulted in such great happiness.

Devata:
The size of the result is not equal to the size of the offering given. Giving is always great. I offered a needle to sew robes. That small offering of a needle became great.

Because of this meritorious deed, I have been born as a very beautiful devata and enjoy all the wonderful things that delight my heart.

Great Bhante, that was the meritorious action I did to have such a beautiful body which shines in all directions.

5.9 Second Needle Mansion

Moggallana Bhante:

Dear Deva, your mansion is way up in the sky and spreads over one hundred and twenty kilometers. Pillars of beryl and other gemstones, and seven hundred pinnacled buildings are in your estate. It is very beautiful. Inside the mansion, you drink and eat and enjoy the sweetness of heavenly food. Guitars play sweet music. You have the five kinds of sensual pleasures. Devatas wearing gold jewelry dance for you.

What are the meritorious deeds that led to this happiness?

Tell me Deva, what kind of meritorious action did you do when you were in the human world to have gained this beauty that shines in all directions, and to have earned all these wonderful things?

That deva, delighted at being questioned by Arahant Moggallana, gladly explained what he had done that resulted in such great happiness.

Deva:

In my previous life, I was a man living in the human world. One day I saw a monk. He was very calm and peaceful. He was a noble monk, free from all defilements. My mind was so happy, and I offered a needle to that Bhante with my own hands.

Because of this meritorious deed, I have been born as a very beautiful deva and enjoy all the wonderful things that delight my heart.

Great Bhante, that was the meritorious action I did to have such a beautiful body which shines in all directions.

5.10 Elephant Mansion

Moggallana Bhante:

Dear Deva, you are sitting on the back of an elephant that travels in the sky using its psychic powers. This all-white elephant has two huge tusks. It is beautifully decorated and very powerful.

On the two tusks are beautiful ponds with crystal clear water and many lotus flowers. In the middle of each lotus, a devata is dancing to divine music.

Oh Deva, you are very powerful even amongst the gods, shining brightly in all directions. What kind of meritorious actions did you do when you were in the human world?

That deva, delighted at being questioned by Arahant Moggallana, gladly explained what he had done that resulted in such great happiness.

Deva:

I offered eight fallen flowers to the stupa that held the relics of the great sage Kassapa Supreme Buddha. I did it with my own hands having a confident mind.

Because of this meritorious deed, I have been born as a very beautiful deva and enjoy all the wonderful things that delight my heart.

Great Bhante, that was the meritorious action I did to have such a beautiful body which shines in all directions.

5.11 Second Elephant Mansion

Vangisa Bhante:

Dear Deva, you are sitting on the back of an elephant that is huge and all white. You travel from park to park, surrounded by goddesses, shining brightly in all directions like the star Osadhi.

What kind of meritorious actions did you do when you were in the human world?

That deva, delighted at being questioned by Arahant Vangisa, gladly explained what he had done that resulted in such great happiness.

Deva:

In my previous life, I was a man in the human world. I was a lay disciple of the All-Seeing Supreme Buddha. I abstained from killing, stealing, taking intoxicants, and lying. I was content with my own wife, and did not even think of other women. I offered things with a very happy mind.

Because of these meritorious deeds, I have been born as a very beautiful deva and enjoy all the wonderful things that delight my heart.

Great Bhante, those were the meritorious deeds I did to have such a beautiful body which shines brightly in all directions.

5.12 Third Elephant Mansion

Man:

Dear Deva, your divine elephant is all white. You are entertained with sweet music. Who are you, traveling on that white elephant in the sky? Are you a god, or a heavenly musician, or the god Sakka? We do not know who you are. We ask you. Tell us the answer.

Deva:

I am not the kind of god that you think, or a heavenly musician, or the god Sakka. I am a god of the Sudhamma clan.

Man:

Worshiping you, Sudhamma, I ask, what meritorious deed did you do to have been born among the Sudhamma gods?

Deva:

Three kinds of houses can be offered: a house made of sugar canes, a house made of grass, or a house made of cloth. Having offered one of these three houses, I was reborn among the Sudhamma gods.

5.13 Small Chariot Mansion

Maha Kaccana Bhante was living in the forest. One day, he saw a prince and spoke to him in this way.

Maha Kaccana Bhante:

You are holding a bow that is made from hardwood, pushing on one end with your foot. Are you a king, a prince, or a hunter in the forest? Who are you?

Prince:

Bhante, I am the son of King Assaka traveling in this forest. I can tell you my name. Everyone knows me as Sujata. I came into this forest looking for deer, but I have not found any. I saw you and stopped here.

Maha Kaccana Bhante:

You have great merit. It is very good that you came here. Your arrival here is not in vain. Take this water and wash your feet. See this cool water I brought from a mountain cave. Drink it and sit on this mat.

Prince:

Great Sage, your words are pleasing, friendly, meaningful, and sweet. Great Ascetic, why do you like to live in this forest? I ask you so that having listened to you and understood, I can follow your Dhamma.

Maha Kaccana Bhante:

Dear Prince, we desire to spread thoughts of harmlessness and compassion towards all living beings. We do not steal, behave badly, or drink alcohol. We abstain from those bad things. Instead we practice the Dhamma, remember much Dhamma, and pay gratitude. These are the things praised in this very life. Truly, these are the things that should be praised.

Oh, dear Prince, listen to me carefully. Within five months, you will die. Before that happens, protect yourself from rebirth in hell.

Prince:

Oh, Bhante, to which country should I run away? What should I do? What kind of effort should I make? What kind of knowledge would help me to escape from this aging and death?

Maha Kaccana Bhante:

Prince, it is impossible to find the place, the effort, or the knowledge by which you can escape from aging and death.

Even kings, those with great wealth and many possessions, are not free from aging and death. Have you heard of soldiers like Andhaka and Venhuputta? Mighty like the sun and moon, they defeated enemies with great strength and bravery, . Eventually when they reached the end of their lifespan they too died.

Kings, brahmins, merchants, servants, and low-caste people – all of them are not free from old age and death. Even those great ascetics, coming from a famous lineage, who had learned spells and many things, are not freed from old age and death.

Other tranquil and virtuous ascetics with austere practices will leave their bodies too when death arrives. Even in the case of Arahants who have completed the path to Nibbana, who are freed from defilements and have overcome both merit and demerit – they too leave this body when the time comes.

Prince:
Great Sage, the Dhamma you preach is very meaningful and well taught. I understood your teaching. Please be my protection. I would go for refuge to you.

Maha Kaccana Bhante:
Dear Prince, do not go for refuge to me. I myself have gone for refuge to the Great Teacher, Gautama Supreme Buddha. You should also go for refuge to that great hero.

Prince:
Oh, Bhante, where is the Great Teacher staying now? I would like to go see the Great Victor, the Unmatchable Teacher.

Maha Kaccana Bhante:
Prince, that excellent teacher who was born in the Okkaka family, lived in the eastern province. Now that Great Teacher attained final Nibbana at passing away.

Prince:

Oh Bhante, if your great teacher was still alive, I would have traveled even for many miles to see him. Bhante, right here, I go for refuge to your great teacher, the Great Hero to whom you have gone for refuge.

I go for refuge to the Supreme Buddha, the excellent Supreme Dhamma, and the Great Teacher's community of monks, the Supreme Sangha. From now on, I abstain from killing, stealing, drinking alcohol, and telling lies. I abstain from sexual misconduct and am content with my own wife.

One day a deva, having dismounted from his divine chariot appeared in front of Maha Kaccana Bhante and paid homage to him.

Maha Kaccana Bhante:

Your chariot travels in the sky shining in all ten directions like the sun that shines with a thousand rays. The chariot is over seventy kilometers long. It is decorated all around with golden plates. Its front is decorated with pearls and gems. Gold and silver carvings beautify your vehicle even further. The head of the chariot is made of beryl gemstones. The yoke is made of red gems. Horses are attached to the chariot with gold and silver ropes. These beautiful horses travel as fast as the mind thinks.

Famous God, you are sitting in this golden chariot pulled by a thousand horses like the god Sakka. I ask you, skilled Deva, how did you gain all these wonderful things?

Deva:

Bhante, in my previous life, I was a prince named Sujata. You were the one who was compassionate towards me and taught me the great Dhamma.

You understood that my life was about to end, gave me a bodily relic of the Supreme Buddha, and told me to worship it. I respected that sacred relic, offering fragrances and flowers respectfully. When I passed away, I was born in this Tavatimsa Heaven in the Nandana Park.

This delightful Nandana Park is filled with various types of birds. I enjoy living there, surrounded by dancing and singing goddesses.

5.14 Great Chariot Mansion

Moggallana Bhante:

Dear Deva, your chariot pulled by a thousand horses is very beautiful and colorful. You are heading to the park sitting on that chariot like the god Sakka, the first giver and the lord of beings. This chariot is made of gold. The bottom edges of the frame are very beautiful. The pillars inside the chariot are well crafted as if they were made by talented artists. The chariot shines like the full moon. This vehicle is covered with golden nets and decorated with various types of jewels. We hear sweet music and see goddesses holding beautiful fly-whisks.

The hub is beautiful as though magically created. Thousands of spokes on the wheel are decorated with gems. The vehicle shines as bright as lightning. This chariot is covered with countless ornaments and has rims with thousands of stripes. Golden nets release the sweet sound of beautiful music. The top is decorated with gems and is as beautiful as the moon. Gleaming, shining, and always pure, it is made even more beautiful with golden carvings. It shines like streaks of beryl gemstones.

These horses are also decorated with jewels like the beautiful moon. They are well built, strong, fast, powerful, and gigantic. They travel to wherever your mind wishes. These four-legged, soft, obedient, pleasing, and pure bred horses move in perfect harmony. As they travel in the sky shaking their ornaments, bells ring and the well-made decorations shine more brilliantly. The voices of these horses are as sweet as music. When the sound of the chariot, the sound of the decorations, the sound of the feet of the horses, the sound of the voices of the horses, and the music of divine musicians are mixed together, it is like an orchestra.

The goddesses in this chariot have extremely beautiful half-closed eyes, like the tender eyes of a deer. They have long eyelashes, smiling faces, and pleasant speech. Their bodies are covered with nets of gems. They are entertained by great heavenly musicians.

These goddesses are decorated with attractive red and gold clothes. They have large, shining, crimson colored eyes. They are worshiping you. These goddesses who have thin waists, thighs, breasts, round fingers, lovely faces, and are decorated with golden ornaments – they are extremely attractive. They are worshiping you.

These goddesses have beautiful braids which are distributed equally and decorated with golden threads. These goddesses are decorated with lotus flowers and are using divine sandalwood cream. They entertain you as you wish. They are worshiping you. Their neck, hands, and legs are decorated with beautiful ornaments. They shine as brilliantly as the sun that shines in all ten directions. The flowers in their hands and their jewelry shake along with the breeze playing sweet music.

Dear Deva, the sounds of chariots, elephants, and birds are heard in your park. Devas who are entertained by these, with lotus-like hands clap and produce the sound of guitars.

When pleasing music is played, very talented goddesses dance, twisting their bodies here and there, on large lotus flowers. When these songs, music, and dances are mixed together, the goddesses dance continuously, shining brightly.

You, fortunate deva, enjoy this sweet music of guitars. You are respected by others like the god Sakka.

What kind of meritorious action did you do when you were in the human world? What kind of precepts did you follow? And what kind of restrained life did you lead? Surely this cannot be the result of a small merit, a small virtue. You are extremely powerful and surpass other gods with your radiance.

Is all this the fruit of your generosity, your virtuous behavior, or because you worshiped monks in the past? Please answer my questions, so that I may know.

That deva, delighted at being questioned by Arahant Moggallana, gladly explained what he had done that resulted in such great happiness.

Deva:
One day, I saw the Great Being who had restrained his senses and freed himself from defilements. He is like the greatest god among all gods, with meritorious marks on his body as if made of gold. He is like a great elephant who crossed over samsara, who opened the doors of deathlessness: Kassapa Supreme Buddha. As soon as I saw the Great Buddha, I made my mind confident

in him. Kassapa Supreme Buddha was a great person who bore the flag of Dhamma and was not attached to anything.

Spreading flowers around my house, I welcomed the Supreme Buddha and offered sweet food, drinks and robes. Yes, I treated the Great Buddha very well with food, drinks, sweets, and robes. Now I travel from heaven to heaven. My home, where my heart delights, is the Sudassana Heavenly Realm.

In that way, I made my mind confident before giving, while giving, and after giving. That is how I practiced meritorious deeds. When I departed from the human world, I was reborn in this heaven, and now I am very happy here like the god Sakka.

Great sage, if someone wishes to enjoy long life, great beauty, happiness and power, they should offer well-arranged food and drinks to the Supreme Buddha who is freed from desires.

Neither in this world nor another world, is there a being greater or equal to the Supreme Buddha. The Supreme Buddha is the worthiest recipient of offerings among all worthy beings. Those who want merit can receive great merit through such offerings.

6. The Payasi Chapter

6.1 Householder's Mansion

Moggallana Bhante:
The best park among all parks is Cittalata Park, found in the great Tavatimsa Heaven. Dear Deva, your mansion shines in the sky like that Cittalata Park.

Powerful Deva, you have become a leader among devas. The pure radiance of your body and limbs is stainless and shines in all directions.

Tell me, what kind of meritorious action did you do when you were in the human world to have gained this beauty that shines in all directions, and to have earned all these wonderful things?

That deva, delighted at being questioned by Arahant Moggallana, gladly explained what he had done that resulted in such great happiness.

Deva:
Bhante, in the human world, my wife and I lived like a pond filled with water – very generously. With confident hearts, we respectfully offered much food and drink to the monks.

Because of this meritorious deed, I have been born as a very beautiful deva and enjoy all the wonderful things that delight my heart.

Great Bhante, that is the meritorious action I did to have such a beautiful body that shines in all directions.

6.2 Second Householder's Mansion

Moggallana Bhante:

The best park among all parks is Cittalata Park, found in the great Tavatimsa Heaven. Dear Deva, your mansion shines in the sky like that Cittalata Park.

Powerful Deva, you have become a leader among devas. The pure radiance of your body and limbs is stainless and shines in all directions.

Tell me, what kind of meritorious action did you do when you were in the human world to have gained this beauty that shines in all directions, and to have earned all these wonderful things?

That deva, delighted at being questioned by Arahant Moggallana, gladly explained what he had done that resulted in such great happiness.

Deva:

Bhante, in the human world, my wife and I lived like a pond filled with water – very generously. With confident hearts, we respectfully offered much food and drink to the monks.

Because of this meritorious deed, I have been born as a very beautiful deva and enjoy all the wonderful things that delight my heart.

Great Bhante, that is the meritorious action I did to have such a beautiful body that shines in all directions.

6.3 Fruit Giver's Mansion

Moggallana Bhante:

This mansion is very high, spreading for one hundred and sixty kilometers, with pillars of beryl and other gemstones. Seven hundred small houses with triangular-shaped roofs are within the complex. This mansion is extremely beautiful.

Dear Deva, inside the mansion, you are drinking and eating. The sweet music of divine guitars plays throughout the complex. Well-trained goddesses delight in dancing and singing.

Powerful Deva, you have become a leader among devas. The pure radiance of your body and limbs is stainless and shines in all directions.

Tell me, what kind of meritorious action did you do when you were in the human world to have gained this beauty that shines in all directions, and to have earned all these wonderful things?

That deva, delighted at being questioned by Arahant Moggallana, gladly explained what he had done that resulted in such great happiness.

Deva:
Great Bhante, if someone offers fruit to the community of noble monks who have pure hearts and calm minds, he will receive a great result. He will enjoy birth in the Tavatimsa Heaven experiencing that great result. Bhante, I too offered four pieces of fruits to the Noble Sangha.

Therefore, the one who wishes happiness in the human world and the heavenly world should offer fruit frequently to the Noble Sangha.

Because of this meritorious deed, I have been born as a very beautiful deva and enjoy all the wonderful things that delight my heart.

Great Bhante, that is the meritorious action I did to have such a beautiful body that shines in all directions.

6.4 Lodging Giver's Mansion

Moggallana Bhante:
Dear Deva, your mansion shines in the sky just as the moon shines brightly, freed from the cover of clouds.

Powerful Deva, you have become a leader among devas. The pure radiance of your body and limbs is stainless and shines in all directions.

Tell me Deva, what kind of meritorious action did you do when you were in the human world to have gained this beauty that shines in all directions, and to have earned all these wonderful things?

That deva, delighted at being questioned by Arahant Moggallana, gladly explained what he had done that resulted in such great happiness.

Deva:
Bhante, in the human world, my wife and I lived like a pond filled with water – very generously. With confident hearts, we respectfully offered lodging to an Arahant along with much food and drink.

Because of these meritorious deeds, I have been born as a very beautiful deva and enjoy all the wonderful things that delight my heart.

Great Bhante, those were the meritorious deeds I did to have such a beautiful body that shines in all directions.

6.5 Second Lodging Giver's Mansion

Moggallana Bhante:
Dear Deva, your mansion shines in the sky just as the sun shines brightly, freed from the cover of clouds.

Powerful Deva, you have become a leader among devas. The pure radiance of your body and limbs is stainless and shines in all directions.

Tell me, what kind of meritorious action did you do when you were in the human world to have gained this beauty that shines in all directions, and to have earned all these wonderful things?

That deva, delighted at being questioned by Arahant Moggallana, gladly explained what he had done that resulted in such great happiness.

Deva:
Bhante, in the human world, my wife and I offered lodging to an Arahant Bhante. With confident hearts, we also respectfully offered much food and drink to the Noble Sangha.

Because of these meritorious deeds, I have been born as a very beautiful deva and enjoy all the wonderful things that delight my heart.

Great Bhante, those were the meritorious deeds I did to have such a beautiful body that shines in all directions.

6.6 Almsfood Giver's Mansion

Moggallana Bhante:
This mansion is very high, spreading for one hundred and sixty kilometers, with pillars of beryl and other gemstones. Seven hundred small houses with triangular-

shaped roofs are within the complex. This mansion is extremely beautiful.

Inside the mansion, you are drinking and eating. The sweet music of divine guitars plays throughout the complex. Well-trained devatas delight in dancing and singing.

Powerful Deva, you have become a leader among devas. The pure radiance of your body and limbs is stainless and shines in all directions.

Tell me, what kind of meritorious action did you do when you were in the human world to have gained this beauty that shines in all directions, and to have earned all these wonderful things?

That deva, delighted at being questioned by Arahant Moggallana, gladly explained what he had done that resulted in such great happiness.

Deva:

In my previous life I lived in the human world. One day, I saw a monk who was very weak and tired from thirst. I offered alms to him and helped him overcome his hunger and thirst.

Because of this meritorious deed, I have been born as a very beautiful deva and enjoy all the wonderful things that delight my heart.

Great Bhante, that is the meritorious action I did to have such a beautiful body that shines in all directions.

6.7 Barley-Warden's Mansion

Moggallana Bhante:
This mansion is very high, spreading for one hundred and sixty kilometers, with pillars of beryl and other gemstones. Seven hundred small houses with triangular-shaped roofs are within the complex. This mansion is extremely beautiful.

Inside the mansion, you are drinking and eating. The sweet music of divine guitars plays throughout the complex. Well-trained devatas delight in dancing and singing.

Powerful Deva, you have become a leader among devas. The pure radiance of your body and limbs is stainless and shines in all directions.

Tell me, what kind of meritorious action did you do when you were in the human world to have gained this beauty that shines in all directions, and to have earned all these wonderful things?

That deva, delighted at being questioned by Arahant Moggallana, gladly explained what he had done that resulted in such great happiness.

Deva:
In my previous life I lived in the human world as the guard of a barley field. One day, I saw an Arahant Bhante who was serene and calm. I offered him a handful of rice with my own hands. Due to the merit of that offering, now I enjoy living in the heavenly Nandana Park.

Because of this meritorious deed, I have been born as a very beautiful deva and enjoy all the wonderful things that delight my heart.

Great Bhante, that is the meritorious action I did to have such a beautiful body that shines in all directions.

6.8 Deva With Decorated Hair Mansion

Moggallana Bhante:
Dear Deva, you are extremely beautiful. You are dressed in beautiful divine clothes. You are wearing divine flower garlands and your hands are decorated with divine ornaments. Most importantly, there are beautiful ornaments in your decorated hair and beard. You are very famous and shine like the moon in your mansion.

The sweet music of divine guitars plays throughout the complex. Well-trained goddesses delight in dancing and singing.

Powerful Deva, you have become a leader among devas. The pure radiance of your body and limbs is stainless and shines in all directions.

Tell me Deva, what kind of meritorious action did you do when you were in the human world to have gained this beauty that shines in all directions, and to have earned all these wonderful things?

That deva, delighted at being questioned by Arahant Moggallana, gladly explained what he had done that resulted in such great happiness.

Deva:
Great Bhante, in my previous life I was in the human world. There I saw virtuous monks who had memorized the Dhamma well and achieved special knowledges. Those Arahant Bhantes were freed from desires and respected by humans and gods. I had confidence in them and I respectfully offered much food and drink.

Because of this meritorious deed, I have been born as a very beautiful deva and enjoy all the wonderful things that delight my heart.

Great Bhante, that is the meritorious action I did to have such a beautiful body that shines in all directions.

6.9 Second Deva With Decorated Hair Mansion

Moggallana Bhante:
Dear Deva, you are extremely beautiful. You are dressed in beautiful divine clothes. You are wearing divine flower garlands and your hands are decorated with divine ornaments. Most importantly, there are beautiful ornaments in your decorated hair and beard. You are very famous and shine like the moon in your mansion.

The sweet music of divine guitars plays throughout the complex. Well-trained devatas delight in dancing and singing.

Powerful Deva, you have become a leader among devas. The pure radiance of your body and limbs is stainless and shines in all directions.

Tell me Deva, what kind of meritorious action did you do when you were in the human world to have gained this beauty that shines in all directions, and to have earned all these wonderful things?

That deva, delighted at being questioned by Arahant Moggallana, gladly explained what he had done that resulted in such great happiness.

Deva:
Great Bhante, in my previous life I was in the human world. There I saw monks with good behavior, who

had memorized the Dhamma well, and achieved special knowledges. Those Arahant Bhantes were freed from desires and respected by humans and gods. I had confidence in them and respectfully offered much food and drink.

Because of this meritorious deed, I have been born as a very beautiful deva and enjoy all the wonderful things that delight my heart.

Great Bhante, that is the meritorious action I did to have such a beautiful body that shines in all directions.

6.10 Uttara's Mansion

Kumara Kassapa Bhante:
Dear Deva, there is a beautiful divine hall owned by the god Sakka called Sudhamma Assembly Hall. All the Devas gather there harmoniously. Shining brilliantly in the sky, your mansion is as beautiful as that assembly hall.

Powerful Deva, you have become a leader among devas. The pure radiance of your body and limbs is stainless and shines in all directions.

Tell me, what kind of meritorious action did you do when you were in the human world to have gained this beauty that shines in all directions, and to have earned all these wonderful things?

That deva, delighted at being questioned by Arahant Kumara Kassapa gladly explained what he had done that resulted in such great happiness.

Deva:

Bhante, in my previous life I lived in the human world as a young servant of King Payasi. I received some money and offered alms using that money. Virtuous monks are very dear to me. I had confidence in them. I offered much food and drink to them respectfully.

Because of this meritorious deed, I have been born as a very beautiful deva and enjoy all the wonderful things that delight my heart.

Great Bhante, that is the meritorious action I did to have such a beautiful body that shines in all directions.

7. The Sunikkhitta Chapter

7.1 Cittalata Mansion

Moggallana Bhante:
The best park among all parks is Cittalata Park, found in the great Tavatimsa Heaven. Dear Deva, your mansion shines in the sky like that Cittalata Park.

Powerful Deva, you have become a leader among devas. The pure radiance of your body and limbs is stainless and shines in all directions.

Tell me, what kind of meritorious action did you do when you were in the human world to have gained this beauty that shines in all directions, and to have earned all these wonderful things?

That deva, delighted at being questioned by Arahant Moggallana, gladly explained what he had done that resulted in such great happiness.

Deva:
In my previous life, I lived in the human world. I was a very poor, helpless servant. I supported my old mother and father. Virtuous monks were very dear to me and I had confidence in them. I respectfully offered them much almsfood.

Because of this meritorious deed, I have been born as a very beautiful deva and enjoy all the wonderful things that delight my heart.

Great Bhante, that is the meritorious action I did to have such a beautiful body that shines in all directions.

7.2 Nandana Mansion

Moggallana Bhante:

The best parks among all parks are Nandana and Cittalata Parks, found in the great Tavatimsa Heaven. Dear Deva, your mansion shines in the sky like those two parks.

Powerful Deva, you have become a leader among devas. The pure radiance of your body and limbs is stainless and shines in all directions.

Tell me Deva, what kind of meritorious action did you do when you were in the human world to have gained this beauty that shines in all directions, and to have earned all these wonderful things?

That deva, delighted at being questioned by Arahant Moggallana, gladly explained what he had done that resulted in such great happiness.

Deva:

In my previous life, I lived in the human world. I was a very poor, helpless servant. I supported my old mother and father. Virtuous monks were very dear to me and I had confidence in them. I respectfully offered them much almsfood.

Because of this meritorious deed, I have been born as a very beautiful deva and enjoy all the wonderful things that delight my heart.

Great Bhante, those were the meritorious actions I did to have such a beautiful body that shines in all directions.

7.3 Mansion with Pillars of Gems

Moggallana Bhante:
Dear Deva, your mansion is very high in the sky and spreads over a hundred and twenty kilometers. There are pillars of beryl and other gemstones, and seven hundred pinnacled buildings in your estate. It is extremely beautiful. Inside the mansion, you drink and eat and enjoy the sweetness of heavenly food. The sweet music of guitars plays. You have many sensual pleasures. Goddesses are dancing and they are wearing golden jewelry.

What are the meritorious deeds that led to this happiness?

Tell me Deva, what kind of meritorious action did you do when you were in the human world to have gained this beauty that shines in all directions, and to have earned all these wonderful things?

That deva, delighted at being questioned by Arahant Moggallana, gladly explained what he had done that resulted in such great happiness.

Deva:
I was in the human world in my previous life. I made a walking path beside a road in a forest. I also planted trees and built a monastery for monks. Virtuous monks were very dear to me and I had confidence in them. I respectfully offered them much almsfood. That is why the pure radiance of my body and limbs is stainless and shines in all directions.

Great Bhante, those were the meritorious actions I did to have such a beautiful body.

7.4 Golden Mansion

Moggallana Bhante:

Dear Deva, your mansion is on a golden mountain and shines brightly. It is covered with nets of gold and ringing bells. Eight-sided pillars made of beryl gemstones and seven other jewels support your mansion. The floor of the mansion is beautiful and made of beryl, gold, crystal, silver, cat's-eyes, pearls, and ruby gems. There is no dust anywhere in the mansion. Golden beams support its pinnacle. There are four stairways facing the four directions. The mansion's inner rooms are made of various jewels and radiate brilliantly like the sun. There are four main stages: one north, one south, one east, one west. They shine throughout the four directions.

You live in this excellent mansion, shining brilliantly like the rising sun. Is all this the fruit of your generosity, your virtuous behavior, or because you worshiped monks in the past? Please answer my questions so that I may know.

That deva, delighted at being questioned by Arahant Moggallana, gladly explained what he had done that resulted in such great happiness.

Deva:

In my previous life, I lived in the human world in the city of Andhakavinda. With a happy mind I built a monastery with my own hands to offer to the Great Teacher, the Kinsman of the Sun, the Supreme Buddha.

I offered that monastery to the Great Teacher along with sweet fragrances, flower garlands, and ointments.

I have received the result of that meritorious deed. Now I am a leader among devas in this Nandana Park. I enjoy living in this park, surrounded by various birds and singing and dancing goddesses.

7.5 Mango Mansion

Moggallana Bhante:
Dear Deva, your mansion is very high in the sky and spreads over a hundred and twenty kilometers. Pillars of beryl and other gemstones, and seven hundred pinnacled buildings are in your estate. It is extremely beautiful. Inside the mansion, you drink and eat and enjoy the sweetness of heavenly food. The sweet music of guitars plays. You have many sensual pleasures. Devas are dancing and they are wearing golden jewelry.

What are the meritorious deeds that you have done to gain this happiness and your position as a leader?

Tell me Deva, what kind of meritorious action did you do when you were in the human world to have gained this beauty that shines in all directions, and to have earned all these wonderful things?

That deva, delighted at being questioned by Arahant Moggallana, gladly explained what he had done that resulted in such great happiness.

Deva:
When I was in the human world, in the last month of the summer, the sun was very hot. There I was the guard of a mango grove and my duty was to watch over the mangoes and water them. One day, the famous Arahant Sariputta Bhante was passing by the mango grove. He appeared to be very tired, although his mind was never tired.

While I was watering the mango trees, I saw Sariputta Bhante approaching the grove. I said, "If I could bathe Bhante, it would lead to my happiness."

Out of pity for me, Sariputta Bhante set aside his outer robes and bowl and sat down in the shade at the foot of a tree wearing his lower robe. I was so delighted. I bathed the Bhante with clean water while he sat there wearing his lower robe. I watered the mango tree and bathed the Bhante at the same time. The merit I collected was not small. My whole body was filled with joy.

That is the only meritorious action I did in the human world. When I passed away, I was reborn in this Nandana Park. I enjoy living in this park, surrounded by various birds and singing and dancing goddesses.

7.6 Cow Herder's Mansion

Moggallana Bhante upon seeing a deva, asked him a question.

Moggallana Bhante:
Dear Deva, you are living in a long-lasting mansion and your hands are decorated with various ornaments. You are mighty and shine like the moon in your mansion.

You are extremely beautiful. You are dressed beautifully in divine clothes. You are wearing divine flower-garlands and your hands are decorated with divine ornaments. Most importantly, beautiful ornaments decorate your hair and beard. You are famous and shine like the moon in your mansion.

The sweet music of divine guitars plays throughout the complex. Well-trained devatas delight in dancing and singing.

Powerful Deva, you have become a leader among devas. The pure radiance of your body and limbs is stainless and shines in all directions.

Tell me Deva, what kind of meritorious action did you do when you were in the human world to have gained this beauty that shines in all directions, and to have earned all these wonderful things?

That deva, delighted at being questioned by Arahant Moggallana, gladly explained what he had done that resulted in such great happiness.

Deva:
In my previous life, I lived in the human world. My job was to gather other people's cows into one place and guard them. One day, a monk approached me on his almsround. At the same time, the cows ran towards a field of beans.

Bhante, suddenly I had to do two things and both had to be done at once. I was wise and realized what I had to do. I dropped my wrapped parcel of rice cake on the ground saying, "Bhante, I offer this to you."

Then I chased after the cows before they damaged the bean field. While I was running, a deadly poisonous snake bit my foot. I was in great pain as I lay there on the ground.

Out of compassion for me, that monk unwrapped the parcel of rice cake and ate it. I died of the snake bite at that moment and was reborn as a deva.

That was the only meritorious action I did. Bhante, it was you who was very compassionate to me. That is why today I experience the happy results of my action.

I know the importance of gratitude, and so, I worship you.

There is no other sage more compassionate than you in this world with its gods and Mara. You are extremely compassionate. I know the importance of gratitude, and so, I worship you.

There is no other sage more compassionate than you in this world or any other worlds. You are extremely compassionate. I know the importance of gratitude, and so, I worship you.

7.7 Kanthaka's Mansion

Moggallana Bhante:

Dear Deva, the mansion in this heaven travels in all directions, shining brightly like the full moon – the leader of stars, surrounded by the constellations. It shines as brightly as the rising sun. Beryl, gold, crystal, silver, cat's-eyes, pearls, and rubies decorate the floor of this mansion. The pillars are extremely beautiful. This mansion is beautifully made.

There is a beautiful lotus pond with many divine fish. It is filled with clear sparkling water, and its bottom is covered in golden sand. Various types of lotuses and white lilies bloom in the pond. When the breeze blows, a sweet fragrance spreads throughout the air. There are two beautiful forests on opposite banks of the pond. Their trees are full of flowers and fruits.

The comfortable chair you are sitting on is made of gold and decorated with divine cloth. You are surrounded by many goddesses, like the god Sakka. Those mighty goddesses, decorated with beautiful ornaments and flowers, entertain you. You are as happy in your mansion as a leader of gods. It is filled with the sweet sounds of drums, conchs, kettle-drums, guitars, and tam-tams. You enjoy the music, dances, and songs. You have received various divine sights, sounds, smells, tastes, and touches. Dear Deva, you shine brighter and brighter in this mansion like the rising sun.

How did you gain all these wonderful things? Is this the result of giving or practicing virtue or paying homage to someone? Please tell me of what meritorious deed this is the result of.

That deva, delighted at being questioned by Arahant Moggallana, gladly explained what he had done that resulted in such great happiness.

Deva:

I lived in the proud city of Kapilavatthu which was owned by the Sakyan people. My name was Kanthaka. I was the dearest horse of Prince Siddhartha, and I was born on the same day as this prince, the son of King Suddhodana.

One day at midnight Prince Siddhartha renounced the palace-life in order to seek enlightenment. He touched my thigh with his soft flexible hands and copper-colored nails. While touching my thigh he told me, "My friend, I am going to achieve enlightenment and after I have attained it, I will help others in the world to cross over this samsara. So carry me, my friend."

I was overjoyed to hear those words. With great delight I let the prince get onto my back. The famous mighty prince sat on my back, and thrilled, I carried him joyfully.

As the sun was rising we approached another kingdom. Leaving me and the chariot-driver Channa, Prince Siddhartha departed silently as if he had no attachment to us.

I licked Prince Siddhartha's sacred feet, with their copper-colored toenails, as he was about to depart. We watched the Great Hero entering the thick forest with tears in our eyes.

As soon as he was out of sight, I suddenly got very ill. Right there and then, I died.

Through the power of that meritorious deed, I have received this heavenly mansion. I enjoy this heaven immensely, surrounded by all the divine pleasures.

One day, other devas were rejoicing, having heard that Prince Siddhartha had attained Supreme Enlightenment. When I heard that, I was overjoyed. Based on that joy, I will attain Nibbana one day.

Bhante, when you approach the Greatest Teacher, the Supreme Buddha, please worship the Blessed One saying, "Deva Kanthaka worships you with his words and by bowing his head."

Soon, I too will go to see the Matchless Teacher who won the battle. It is extremely rare to see such a Supreme Buddha, who is unshaken by the ups and downs of the world. He is the true protector of the world.

On a later day, recollecting the help of the Great Teacher, and feeling grateful and thankful for his teachings, Deva Kanthaka went to see the Supreme Buddha. Having listened to the Buddha's teaching, he understood it and gained the Eye of Dhamma.

Deva Kanthaka removed self-centered view, doubt, and wrongful practices and became a Stream Entrant. After worshiping the Supreme Teacher's sacred feet, he disappeared right there and then.

7.8 Mansion of Many Colors

Moggallana Bhante:

Dear Deva, your body is multicolored. You are in a colorful mansion without sadness, surrounded by goddesses. You experience delight, like the god Sunimmita. No one equals your fame, merit, strength, and psychic power. All the devas in Tavatimsa Heaven are gathered here worshiping you, just as people worship the moon. Goddesses are dancing, singing, and entertaining you.

Powerful Deva, you have become a leader among devas. You shine brilliantly in all directions. Tell me Deva, what kind of meritorious action did you do when you were in the human world to have gained this beauty that shines in all directions, and to have earned all these wonderful things?

That deva, delighted at being questioned by Arahant Moggallana, gladly explained what he had done that resulted in such great happiness.

Deva:

Bhante, at that time, there was a Supreme Buddha named Sumedha Buddha. I was a disciple of that great victor. Even though I was a monk for seven years near the Buddha, I did not attain any stage of enlightenment. I lived just as an ordinary monk.

Sumedha Supreme Buddha, the Great Teacher, the Great Victor, the one who is unshaken by ups and downs, attained final Nibbana at passing away. A stupa, of a golden net and decorated with gems, was built to hold the Buddha's sacred relics. I worshiped that stupa with a happy mind.

Although I did not have anything with which to practice generosity, I encouraged others. I would tell people, "Pay homage to the sacred relics of the Buddhas, who are worthy of homage, and you will be able to go to heaven!"

That was the only meritorious action I did. From the result of that, I enjoy this divine happiness rejoicing in the midst of Tavatimsa devas. The result of that meritorious deed has not yet ended.

7.9 Mattakundali's Mansion

A Brahmin was crying over his dead son's grave when he saw a grieving deva who was disguised as a young man.

Brahmin:

My dear child, you are very handsome, wearing polished earrings, garlands, and sandalwood cream. You are weeping, holding your head in your hands in the middle of this forest. Why are you crying so sadly?

Deva:

I have received a bright golden chariot, but it does not have wheels. That is why I am so sad. I am about to commit suicide.

Brahmin:

Oh dear boy, tell me, what kind of wheels do you need? Should they be made of gold, jewels, rubies, or silver? I will give you a pair of wheels made from anything.

Deva:

We can see the sun and moon right here. It would be great if my chariot could have them as wheels.

Brahmin:

Oh, dear boy, you are indeed foolish. You seek something that cannot be obtained. I am sure that you will die from sadness because it is impossible to get the sun and moon as your wheels.

Deva:

But wait a minute. We can see the sun and moon moving in the sky. We can see their color and tracks. But when someone dies, one can never see him again. So, who is more foolish, you or me? You are crying over your dead son, who cannot even be seen, and I am crying over something that can at least be seen.

Brahmin:

Oh, dear boy, what you just said is very true. Of the two of us I am the greater fool. I am crying to get my dead son back, like a childish boy crying to obtain the moon.

My heart was burning with sadness over the death of my son, like when ghee is poured onto a fire. But now, all my sorrow has been extinguished as if I had been sprayed with water. I was struck with an arrow of grief, but you have removed it from me, my dear boy. Having heard your advice, I have become tranquil and cool, with the arrow of sorrow removed. I no longer grieve or weep.

Are you a god, a divine musician, the god Sakka, or someone's son? Who are you?

Deva:

Your son has been cremated in this cemetery. You are weeping over his remains. I am that son of yours. Having done a meritorious deed, I was reborn in the Tavatimsa Heaven as a deva.

Brahmin:

We have never known you to give a small or large gift in charity. We have never known you to observe the Five or Eight Precepts. What kind of meritorious action did you do to go to heaven?

Deva:

Do you remember when I was very sick and lying sadly on a bed outside our house? One day, all of a sudden, I saw the Supreme Buddha who had great wisdom and a pure mind, and who had realized everything about this world.

I was very happy and had confidence when I saw him. I quickly worshiped him. That was the only meritorious action I did to have come to this heaven.

Brahmin:

It is wonderful! Just mere worshiping has resulted in a great happiness. Without delay, on this very day, I happily place confidence in the Buddha. I go for refuge to the Buddha.

Deva:

That is exactly what you should do. From this very day, go for refuge to the Supreme Buddha, the Supreme Dhamma, and the Supreme Sangha with a confident mind. Follow the Five Precepts honestly without breaking any of them.

Stop killing any beings, never steal, never drink alcohol, never lie, never commit sexual misconduct, and be content with your own wife.

Brahmin:

Oh Deva, you really wish for my well-being. You have been very helpful to me. From today onward, you are my teacher. I will do all the things you advised me to do. With a confident mind I go for refuge to the Supreme Buddha, the excellent Dhamma, and the disciples of the Great Teacher – the Noble Sangha. I will stop killing living beings, never steal anything, never drink alcohol, never lie, and never commit sexual misconduct. I will be content with my own wife.

7.10 Serissaka's Mansion

A meeting took place between the deva Serissaka and some merchants. Please listen to this good story they told.

There was a king named Payasi in the city of Setavya. He was reborn as an earth deva. He lives happily in his mansion. That deva spoke to the merchants.

Deva:

Non-humans live in frightening forests and in deserts where there is little food, drink, and water. Your journey through this desert is very hard. You are about to die in the middle of this sandy place.

In this desert, there are no fruits, roots or any food or drink. There is no way to make a fire. There is only dust and scorching sand. This rough soil is like a scorched iron pot. It is like hell, without any happiness. This place has been haunted by ghosts for a long time. It seems that this land is under a curse of rishis. What are you seeking? Why have you come here? Is it because of greed, or fear, or have you gotten lost?

Merchants:

Dear Deva, we are merchants from the cities of Magadha and Anga. We travel with full carts to the cities of Sindhu and Sovira to earn money.

We could not stand the heat in the daytime. So, looking for a comfortable place for ourselves and out of compassion for our bulls, we rushed here to this place.

We took the wrong road in the night. We are lost and confused like blind men lost in a forest. We do not know where to go. We are stuck in the middle of this desert.

Deva, we have not seen anything like your mansion before. It is excellent. Because we have seen you, we are extremely happy. It is as if we have regained our lives.

Deva:

People travel to lands on the other side of the oceans. They travel through sandy deserts, over bridges made of canes and stakes, and to many more difficult places just to earn money. When you travel to different countries, what kind of things do you see and hear? I would like to learn about those strange things.

Merchants:

Deva, we have never seen or heard about any happiness greater than yours. Your happiness surpasses human happiness in every way. No matter how long we stare, we will never see enough of your mansion. There are pools in the sky with many white lotuses. The surrounding area is filled with trees that do not stop bearing fruit. Divine fragrance can be smelled everywhere. Your mansion is supported by hundreds of pillars made of beryl, crystals, corals, cat's-eye, rubies, and brilliant jewels. There are golden stages decorated with golden railings.

This mansion shines in gold and it is well designed with beautiful stairs. It is extremely beautiful.

There is lots of food and drink inside. Many goddesses play musical instruments and sing welcoming songs to entertain you. You enjoy being surrounded by these goddesses. The happiness you experience is beyond words. It is like the wonderful Nalini Palace of King Vessavana. Are you a god, a demon, the god Sakka, or a human? We merchants question you. Tell us who you are.

Deva:
Dear merchants, I am a deva. My name is Serissaka. I am the protector of this sandy desert. I was appointed by King Vessavana.

Merchants:
Deva, have you obtained these wonderful things by chance, have you created them yourself, or have other gods given them to you? How did you gain all these delightful things?

Deva:
Merchants, I did not obtain these wonderful things by chance, nor did I create them myself. Other devas did not give them to me. I have obtained these things as a result of my own meritorious deeds.

Merchants:
Dear Deva, what kind of religious activities did you perform and what kind of precepts did you follow? What kind of good deed did you do to gain these wonderful things.

Deva:

I was once a ruler in the country Kosala. My name was Payasi. I held the wrong view that there are no results of good and bad actions. I was very greedy and evil. I believed that nothing exists after death.

There was a great monk named Kumara Kassapa who knew the Supreme Buddha's Dhamma well and could preach skillfully. One day, that monk taught me the Dhamma. That was the day he removed my terrible wrong views.

After hearing his sermon, I became a lay follower of the Supreme Buddha. I abstained from killing beings, stealing, drinking alcohol, lying, and was content with my own wife. That was my religious life and those were the precepts I followed. Due to those meritorious deeds, I obtained this wonderful mansion.

Whatever teaching has been preached by the wise is true. Those teachings are not false. Good doers enjoy the results of their actions wherever they go. Evil doers experience grief, lamentation, and misery wherever they go. They will never escape from falling into miserable worlds.

At that moment, the assembly of devas suddenly became very frightened and sad.

Merchants:

Dear Deva, what happened to you and your fellow devas? Why do you suddenly seem sad?

Deva:

Dear merchants, can you see these flowering Mahari trees in this forest spreading divine fragrance and dispelling darkness? After every hundred years, one petal of each flower falls off. That indicates that we devas have been here for one hundred years. I will stay in this mansion only for five hundred years. I know that very well. By then, my life span and merit will be spent. That is why I am very sad.

Merchants:

Dear Deva, having obtained a wonderful, long lasting mansion like yours, what is the point of being sad? If someone has a short lifespan and little merit it makes sense for them to be sad.

Deva:

Dear merchants, you advised me using pleasing words with good hearts. I will protect you. You will be able to go safely to your destination.

Merchants:

We wish to go to the cities of Sindhu and Sovira to earn money. We promise that we will organize a huge ceremony in the name of Serissaka with lots of gifts.

Deva:

Do not organize ceremonies for me. You will get everything you wish for without having to reward me. Stop doing evil deeds and lead a virtuous life.

There is a lay follower of the Buddha in your group. He is very faithful, virtuous, generous, wise, and well-behaved. He is learned in the Dhamma. He is a very happy lay follower with deep wisdom.

He does not tell lies intentionally. He does not even think to kill beings. He does not try to break others' friendships, and he speaks beneficial things wisely. He is very disciplined, obedient, and established in higher virtue. He respects elders and looks after his parents.

He has great noble qualities. I think he earns money just to take care of his parents, not to make himself rich. He intends to be a monk after his parents pass away.

He is straight, not crooked, and not deceitful. How could he experience suffering since he is well established in good qualities?

It is because he was in your group that I appeared before you. Therefore, merchants, following the Dhamma is the best protection. If you had come without that lay follower, you could have been destroyed by disasters in this desert like confused blind men. Association with good people is indeed a blessing.

Merchants:

Deva, please tell us, who is that person? What is his name? What is his role among us? We agree that if you appeared here out of compassion for someone, his company is truly a blessing.

Deva:

Yes, he is a servant of yours. He is your barber, Sambhava. He earns money shaving and cutting people's hair. Recognize him as that lay follower. He is a very quiet person. Don't look down upon him.

Merchants:

Dear Deva, we know who you are talking about. We never thought he was such a person. Having heard your praises, we are ready to worship him.

Deva:

Everybody traveling with you – elders, youth, children, and anyone who is greedy, come inside my mansion and see well the results of merits.

Placing the barber in the front, they all rushed behind him saying, "I am next! I am next!" They went inside the mansion as if entering the wonderful palace of the god Sakka.

When it was time to go for refuge, they all cried, "Let me go first!" wanting to become lay disciples of the Supreme Buddha. They abstained from killing, stealing, drinking alcohol, lying, and were content with their own wives. Everyone rejoiced in taking refuge in the Triple Gem. They rejoiced again and again enjoying divine wonders.

Afterwards, they went to Sindhu and Sovira safely and accomplished their goal of making lots of money. They eventually returned to their home city of Pataliputta safely. They went to their own houses, rejoined their wives and children, and organized a great festival called Serissaka. They delighted in this festival together with their families. They also built an assembly hall called Serissaka.

This is the result of association with noble friends, people who practice the Dhamma. Because of a single lay follower a large group of people benefited.

7.11 Sunikkhitta's Mansion

Moggallana Bhante:
Dear Deva, this mansion is very high, spreading for a hundred and twenty kilometers. There are pillars of beryl and other gemstones. Seven hundred small houses with triangular-shaped roofs are within the complex. This mansion is extremely beautiful.

Inside the mansion, you are drinking and eating. The sweet music of divine guitars plays throughout the complex. Well-trained devatas delight in dancing and singing.

Powerful Deva, you have become a leader among devas. The pure radiance of your body and limbs is stainless and shines in all directions.

Tell me, what kind of meritorious action did you do when you were in the human world to have gained this beauty that shines in all directions, and to have earned all these wonderful things?

That deva, delighted at being questioned by Arahant Moggallana, gladly explained what he had done that resulted in such great happiness.

Deva:

Some flowers that had been offered to the stupa of the Supreme Buddha had been scattered here and there. I arranged those flowers beautifully while recollecting the great qualities of the Supreme Buddha. Now I enjoy heavenly pleasures and have great power and might.

Because of this meritorious deed, I have been born as a very beautiful deva and enjoy all the wonderful things that delight my heart. The radiance of my body shines in all directions. Great Bhante, that was the meritorious action I did when I was in the human world.

Mahamegha English Publications

- **Transalated Dhamma Books**

1. The Wise Shall Realize
2. Stories of Ghosts from the Petavatthu
3. Stories of Heavenly Mansions from the Vimanavatthu

- **Translated Picture Storybooks**

1. The Life of Buddha for Children
2. Chaththa Manawaka
3. Sumana the Novice Monk
4. Stingy Kosiya of Town Sakkara
5. Kisagothami

Mahamegha Publishers - Polgahawela

Tel : 037 2053300, 0773 216685 e-mail : mahameghapublishers@gmail.com

Thipitaka Sadaham Poth Madura - Borella

Tel : 0114 255 987, 077 4747161 e-mail : thripitakasadahambooks@gmail.com

Printed in Great Britain
by Amazon

50125222R00090